WHAT PEOPLE ARE SAYING ABOUT

High Love -

Amidst the heartbreak of losing ~~~~ Winnie, Andrew found comfort and solace in the ways that her spirit spoke to him. Messages from his departed wife found their way across the divide between this realm and the next. As Andrew recounts his heartfelt journey, his book serves as a reminder that those we love are only a thought a way.
Denise Linn, author of *Signposts*

Told from the heart, Andrew Bentley's book offers evidence aplenty that the so-called dead continue to exist in a higher realm and nothing can sever the bond of love. Andrew provides proof that survival after death is a living reality and those Beyond likewise provide meaningful signs and signals they are still very much around. *High Love – Still Connected* will bring comfort, calm, hope and healing to all who read it.
Tony Ortzen, Editor, *Two Worlds*

Andrew Bentley offers a heartfelt and moving story about life, death, and unconditional love from the Afterworld. As I read this book, the only word I could think of that describes the relationship between this husband and wife, is LOVE. *High Love – Still Connected* is a marvelous depiction of proof of life after death. Winnie's warmth and compassion for her family and friends is a pristine example of how loved ones departed never leave those they left behind. Her signs prove that even in death, LOVE conquers and continues to grow.
Lyn Ragan, author of *Wake Me Up! How Chip's Afterlife Saved Me From Myself*

Moving and passionate – an amazing story that highlights the true power of love.
Emily Haddington, Editor, *Soul & Spirit*

High Love
– Still Connected

High Love
– Still Connected

Andrew Bentley

Winchester, UK
Washington, USA

First published by Sixth Books, 2017
Sixth Books is an imprint of John Hunt Publishing Ltd., Laurel House, Station Approach,
Alresford, Hants, SO24 9JH, UK
office1@jhpbooks.net
www.johnhuntpublishing.com
www.6th-books.com

For distributor details and how to order please visit the 'Ordering' section on our website.

ISBN: 978 1 78535 411 3
978 1 78535 578 3 (ebook)
Library of Congress Control Number: 2016954751

A CIP catalogue record for this book is available from the British Library.

Design: Stuart Davies

Printed and bound by CPI Group (UK) Ltd, Croydon, CR0 4YY, UK

We operate a distinctive and ethical publishing philosophy in all areas of our business, from our global network of authors to production and worldwide distribution.

CONTENTS

For my angel, my everything, my forever...

Acknowledgements

There are so many family and friends notably in Britain, Belgium, Australia, Switzerland, France, Germany and Singapore who have helped me, and not only with this book. They supported me through the darkest times after losing my wonderful wife. I thank all those who were there from the beginning, some of whom are already mentioned in the book, sharing in the developing events, reading drafts, giving invaluable opinions, and encouraging me to go ahead and act on what my instinct told me. Thanks to the team at John Hunt Publishing/6th Books. They were the only publisher I contacted; it just felt right. Love and gratitude most of all to my daughters, who have kept me moving forward by simply needing and deserving the best dad that I can be.

Introduction

'De verbondenheid, eenheid, liefde.' These were the words in Dutch, meaning connection, unity, and love, that my Belgian wife Winnie wrote in one of her pocket notebooks about eight months before she died aged forty-seven, completely unexpectedly. She was referring to our relationship, and I was reading her words for the first time a few months after she tragically passed away, having discovered the precious little book among some of her belongings.

Now, two years on from the late summer of 2013, I feel compelled to tell you our story, one of how love survives, even grows to another level, and can uplift and heal us. I want to take you through the significant different phases of our lives together, to understand our harmony. From the origins and development as a couple, then the life-changing five-week period up to her death. This is followed by stories and accompanying photos of what has been happening since: the many loving signs and messages, some would say coincidences, that my family, friends and I have received, and are so grateful for. I believe that very many people have sensed such signs of great personal meaning, but possibly have been unable or unwilling to talk about them outside their normal circles. I just want to share our experiences with you, taking a holistic view of the key events to best convey their significance and wider context. The story of one sign in isolation is a world away from reading about the big picture, made up of many pieces that seemingly fit together to create a mystic jigsaw. Right from when Winnie died, it felt completely natural for me to talk to people and be open about it, sometimes even with relative strangers. I just followed my instinct, which has invariably served me well. And so this is how I've written it, telling the stories mostly as if you're sat in front of me, in an attempt to present some perceptions of deep and complex implication in an accessible way.

My sincere hope is that this book will give comfort, hope and strength to people who have lost loved ones (or for that matter anyone who is just curious to hear a true story about love, life and beyond), to encourage people to take time to reflect on the possibility that loved ones' spirits live on and are still close by and thriving.

Recognising that we will all endure both light and darkness in our lives, it's so important to cherish all that we have, to live in the moment, to rise in the sunshine, to strengthen us for the times of shadow. Growing up, I had always imagined being in a profession helping people, be it a teacher or in a hospital in some capacity. However, for various reasons, this never happened, and my career followed another path. I see this book as the opportunity to fulfil that wish, albeit in an unusual and wholly unexpected manner. In much the same way, there was a nebulous kind of thought and feeling about myself and Winnie as a couple, that together we were capable of making some kind of small difference, something altruistic, but not knowing how. So I think of this book as the two of us hoping to open eyes.

I suspect everyone has these gut feelings about what might lie ahead? I have always listened to those 'messages' coming from somewhere deep in our consciousness. And to seemingly underline this 'collaboration', at the time of writing the chapter 'Before', I decided it was time to look into Winnie's Belgian pension documents. In doing so, I came across many letters and emails between us from years ago that she had kept, and that have helped me to relive those times and special moments.

Writing this book is not at all about individual gain or for some kind of recognition. Any personal profits generated will be gifts to charity. I'm not a medium, I don't adhere to any particular religious beliefs, and have no intention to be divisive or upset anyone by sharing my experiences, insights and interpretations. I'm just a forty-eight year old man from Yorkshire, who has been incredibly lucky to have found the most wonderful partner imaginable, with whom I still have a special bond, and who continues to show her love since passing on. It's so fortunate that my recollections of our life and the emotions at the exact moments described come so effortlessly, and with such clarity. My goal is not to try to convince readers about the notion of the afterlife. It's to have an open mind about what we've experienced, shared with you in the following pages. I asked myself, 'Is it enough just to believe in something after this tragedy happened, or can you do more to change things for the better?' The thought of a book was daunting at first and of doubtful value outside our family and friends. But I realised at a certain moment that such positive changes have to start from the smallest beginnings by individuals driven by belief and intuition, striving to make a difference. Some people's loss inspires them to raise money for relevant charities by climbing mountains, running marathons or riding challenging distances. My tribute to Winnie through positive action is to raise awareness.

After the truly devastating loss of my 'special one', it's difficult to communicate just how much the signs and the subsequent reflection and belief have uplifted me. I believe that Winnie has somehow opened up previously untapped inner strength, clarity and depth of thought, and intuition that I never knew existed in me. Where this came from, I don't know, but it makes me think of tips of icebergs… it has helped me to understand what really matters, how to appreciate all that we have, and to live every moment. No longer is anything taken for granted, and I have found greater purpose. Life and the world have perspective, and make more sense to me now – what we're doing here, what it's all for. In a way, I have discovered who I really am, deep below the surface, all emanating from the enduring love of Winnie Jane Bentley.

I will always refer to this as 'Winnie's book', which I find somehow apt because I wrote personal ones for my two lovely daughters about the first six years of their lives, and called them 'the girls' books'. There is a certain symmetry to this too – the girls' books were for them to delight in knowing about themselves and their early lives before they could recall. Winnie's book suggests that there are important things that we are not able to consciously know or remember about existence and our true selves. In both cases, they are written for love. When I often told Winnie that I loved her, she would sometimes cheekily and abruptly challenge me 'Why?', instead of just accepting the familiar and inadequate trio of words. Put on the spot, I endeavoured to present various good reasons and examples in the hope of satisfying her. However, I never believed that my efforts quite did justice to what I felt and feel for Winnie, and so I would like to think that this book will help me to succeed at long last, and for the message to find its way home…

Chapter 1

Before

In the late 1990s, I was living and working in Belgium, going through a very difficult marriage. A clash of fundamental values and upbringing were at the core of our problems, and though I can say that my ex-wife and I are now on good terms, being the proud parents of two daughters, it was an extremely challenging time for both of us. In my case, under the cloak and mask of outward serenity and total denial, inside I had utterly lost the sense of who I was, and what I stood for. In truth, we were an incompatible partnership, and the relationship was sadly descending into paralysis. But I can truly say that there are no regrets, I listened to my heart even though I immediately knew our relationship would be demanding, and she has been an important part of my life. We did have good times together, and learned vital lessons about each other. Without her, we would not have our children, and the future connection with Winnie would have been an extremely unlikely scenario, almost certainly out of reach. *Some things do appear to happen for a reason...*

I met Winnie Vanderhaegen on my first day at work at a new company, in October 1998. I call this the luckiest day of my life. There were no notable sparks between us in that first encounter. She was friendly, helpful and welcoming, as you would hope from a new colleague. However, looking back on those first moments, I do remember an immediate feeling of trust, and instinctive recognition of a good and true person behind her subtly mischievous smile and mellow, resonant voice.

It would be more than two years later that Winnie Jane (as I mostly called her) and I became a couple. Quite simply, her friendship and then her courage and love saved my life. Having been completely lost, and as low as I've ever been, she somehow could see what I couldn't in myself. My very being had been on the verge of disintegrating but she healed me, and helped to put me back together into a far more positive, confident and truer version of the original. *And, as strange and even alien as it may seem, I'm yet stronger after her passing, somehow fortified by her love and belief in me – more to come on this later...*

When in her company, all my senses were somehow heightened and more alert, as if she transferred life energy to me. We shared almost a telepathic understanding of one another's moods, thoughts and needs, so in tune were we. *What it feels like to be in love...* she was a priceless 'gift' in so many ways, our paths intersecting at exactly the time when we both needed it most in our lives. *Ever since, I feel that our two paths still run together, even now.* Honestly, I don't believe it would have been possible for me to find a more beautiful and better matching partner had I met the entire eligible female population on the planet. It felt as though all the events through my life and the thousands of decisions taken and the choices made were designed for me to arrive at that very point to be with Winnie. We both said that we would not have been ready for each other had we met earlier in our lives. *Maybe most people would conclude the same about the unique circumstances and timing that brought them together with their partner?*

We recognised how lucky we were to have found each other, like we had won the lottery, such a slim chance to be with the one who matches so naturally. My most precious photo of Winnie is also a kind of gift, a reminder of the genesis of our bond. It was taken by a colleague on what I recognised to be the day when the tiniest seed of our future relationship was planted. A day in which something intangible, mysterious and unnerving passed between us on such a subtle, almost subconscious level, like our souls already knew something that we didn't, but we both felt it, I later learned.

One of the most momentous single events of my life was the first time that our hands joined. An energy shock channelled up my arm and through my whole body the moment that my hand found hers. Long hidden treasure had been discovered, a secret code unearthed, an alignment of our beings. The message was deafeningly loud and of overwhelming clarity. In fact, touch was a vital part of our 'recipe' to stay emotionally close during all the years we were together, and often transmitted our feelings better than any words could ever do. When we embraced, I remember the sensation of the connection of our hearts, beating together, bound together, drawn closer by a profound natural magnetism that always remained. A gravitational pull of pure emotion, like planet and moon that had always existed together in harmony. *And it still feels like this...*

Winnie was one of those rare people who was admired without jealousy, liked and loved by virtually everyone who met her. She was not just highly intelligent and proficient in every-thing she did, speaking five languages fluently and with a born perfectionist's discerning eye for detail. She had an amazing innate talent for communicating and bonding with people from all cultures. People naturally felt positive and calm around her, and this allowed her to build wonderful lifelong friendships. Being around her was like getting a fix of 'soul food', she somehow gave you energy, not like some who strip it away by simply being in their presence. Always ready to laugh, I was not the only one to be mesmerised by the smile in her beautifully pure eyes. People were proud to call Winnie a friend, and she was always ready to help in any situation, either in a practical way, or just by listening and talking things through. She touched the fortunate few who knew her, their lives enhanced and changed for the better. She loved to cook for loved ones, a student of world cuisine, a different delicious dish almost every day. As much as she was fascinated by, and had respect for, other cultures, she was a very proud Belgian. In her mind, no other beers came close, and she had a keen sense of indignation when she perceived any unfair slight against her country. *And I smile at the memory of her annoyance when, like the UK, Belgium scored poorly (unfairly in her view) in the Eurovision Song Contest!*

Winnie Jane was the most generous and committed stepmum and role model, giving up so much of her life in Belgium to be with me and my daughters in England. The girls were truly loved, just like they were her own. Her nature and character were a wondrous, balanced, irresistible blend of kindness and steel, pragmatism and creativity, shyness and competence, wisdom and frivolity, grace and determination, head and heart...

Winnie's parents were a huge part of her life, and an inspiration to her. They had a wonderfully close and constructive relationship, instilling into their only child the values of respect, hard work, love of family, and appreciation of the everyday things in life. This was very much in common with the relationship I have with my own parents and three brothers. Winnie's papa, Pierre, was an affable, steadying influence full of humour, mischief and wisdom. Nelly, Winnie's mama, is an altogether different character of courage and will, intuition, kindness and the occasional bout of stubbornness. She is also one of the most naturally funny people I've ever had the pleasure to meet. Winnie was brought up as a Catholic, as most children are in Belgium. However, she was not particularly religious and as an adult developed an interest in spiritual and related matters such as karma, life after death, reincarnation, astrology, and dreams. When we occasionally discussed these subjects, she mentioned 'moving to a higher level' a number of times. I admit that at the time, I didn't really understand what this meant, but she has opened my eyes now, as I'll explain in the next chapters.

Even as an adult, Winnie had always lived nearby her parents and was able to see them every day, so it was a painful wrench to leave them to be with me, for which I can never thank her enough. An immeasurable debt of gratitude is also owed to

Pierre, when Winnie, unbeknown to me, had some last minute doubts about the wisdom of following her heart down this risky and uncertain path ahead of her. I believe her father saw how happy his beloved daughter was, and selflessly advised in his calm way to take the jump, reassuring her that she could always rebuild her life back in Belgium, should it not work out.

Winnie really did change her life completely to make all this happen, leaving her stable and challenging job in Belgium, driven to work tirelessly on the daunting task of independently finding work in a foreign country. This was so important, not just for her to settle into life in England, but also a vital financial need due to the high maintenance payments I had to honour at the time. Love alone couldn't put food on the table or give our fledgling partnership a fighting chance under such circumstances. Thankfully, all worked out well, and she secured a job before she moved in June 2001, the company that employed her being smart enough to recognise a sparkling and special jewel when they found one. Winnie and I saw her parents as often as we could, the route between Belgium and England becoming a well-travelled journey for the four of us. They spoke daily on the phone to maintain the constant contact that was a feature of their family life.

All through our time together, Winnie and I were always open and honest with each other and ourselves, always sharing our thoughts and concerns when there were problems, learning, adapting and developing in unison. There were plenty of challenges to deal with that threatened to undermine us, mainly borne of frustration from the continuing effects of the strained relationship with my ex-wife. At times, Winnie could have easily decided to quit and return to Belgium, and I would not have blamed her. But she was so courageous and had such positive conviction, sticking by me because we instinctively knew that we belonged together, and our bond was unbreakable, whatever happened to us. Confronting the challenges as one and knowing that we were coming home to each other every day made it all worthwhile.

I saw first-hand how difficult and complex it can be to be a stepmother. So many conflicting internal and external factors and emotions, battling for acceptance, confusion and insecurity never far away. The opposite end of the pendulum's arc told of a different story. The joy of being an integral and constant part of the lives of two girls from very young ages touched her deeply. She took her supporting role and responsibility very seriously, and she was able to be a little more objective than me in many important matters like respect and behaviour. She had a lovely way of providing a calm home environment every weekend when they stayed with us, ensuring that everything ran smoothly: caring, consistent and organised. Winnie always understood and maintained that the girls' interests had to come first, never once complaining about nor regretting the choice she made to be with us. My parents and brothers recognised almost immediately how vital Winnie was to both me and my daughters, and felt they had been gifted with a daughter and sister. A modern day angel... in one of her notebooks, she wrote, 'I'm grateful to have the girls, and privileged to be able to help them, to show the way.'

When we were first together, Winnie's attitude to marriage was one of apathy. She just didn't see what difference a piece of paper made to a healthy union that already happily existed. However, her outlook changed over time the more settled our lives had become – she had found her home. Four years after arriving in England, in June 2005, Winnie and I were married in a very simple and intimate ceremony. I call this the best single thing that I ever did. It felt so destined, like finally arriving home after embarking on a lifelong quest. *The first morning after, emerging from an exquisite slumber beside Winnie as her husband, smiling sleepily to myself as I blinked at my new ring with pride...*

The foundations of our bond were deep and immovable. The

bricks used to build our house, sturdy and aligned. Marriage served to bind all this together to create a kind of force field, a belief that we could meet and withstand any challenge that would be encountered. It was heartening to learn that our friends could sense the connection we had too. On the wedding day of a couple who were some of our best friends, they said, 'We want to be like you two!' Another childhood friend, Darren, who is very perceptive, observed, 'It's like you are the same, with no distinct male and female role' (as if we interchange and match so well).

However, no couple can be 'perfect', and there were plenty of mistakes, committed almost exclusively by me, to be truthful. Winnie's standards in almost everything she did were consistently, exasperatingly (and sometimes annoyingly) high. From household chores, cooking a sauce for dinner, planning holidays, and remembering birthdays to major projects at work, she had to give her best, and was not happy if she fell short. Alas, the opportunities for me to redress the balance a little by solemnly but playfully bringing to her attention some small error she had made were incredibly few. Sometimes, she forgot to turn off the shower switch in the bathroom. Hardly a big deal.

Tragically, a devastating change was just around the corner. A matter of five months after the wedding, Winnie's dad was diagnosed with lung cancer. Four months later, sadly he was gone, but his dignity, bravery and sense of humour were intact until the end. I can say now that Winnie was never quite the same again. For someone so in touch with her feelings and her mind, she was mostly unable to talk about the shock and pain of losing her dad. She would fall apart if she confronted all the hurt, she told me. It was the one thing that was almost off limits for us. Not a day went by without Pierre touching her thoughts, and she knew that he lived in her, in that they were so alike, not just in character but also their eyes, looking back at her in the mirror every day. However, she wasn't able to share her feelings of grief (in direct contrast to her husband!). On reflection, it's astonishing that for a couple that believed in the afterlife, never once did spirituality enter into the conversations about Pierre, and I often think this was a missed opportunity that could have gone some way to healing Winnie's heart.

Winnie's main concern was her mum, and the mental struggle of not being physically there for her during the darkest and most sombre times. Her parents had been together, also working in their own patisserie, for forty-two years, and had barely spent a night apart in all that time. You could only smile to see them together. Thankfully, Nelly was extremely well cared for by her extended family in Belgium, which was a comforting relief to Winnie. No daughter could have done more to help her mother through the anguish together; it was both touching and bruising to witness their love and shared loss. *That was my Winnie, she gave everything of herself...*

For all the years after her dad's passing, Winnie and her mum were in constant contact, dealing as best they could with the dual obstacles of distance and emptiness. On returning home from work, it was traditionally Winnie's first action of the evening to call her mum, aperitif in hand, to discuss the day's happenings, which improved my comprehension of Dutch no end! The passing of time helped them to find more balance and peace, with little bitterness or self-pity, and their mutual love and appreciation grew yet deeper. Winnie had always given so much for the girls and I, motivating me to be equally determined to do the same for her and Nelly – what families are for of course...

Winnie and I always shared the same philosophy about life, and encouraged the girls to follow our lead – appreciate the little everyday things, and you'll be happy. We took pleasure from every single meal together, a glass of wine, a heart to heart conversation walking in the countryside, Sunday siestas, a beautiful sunrise while driving to work, a kind smile from a stranger... when things became financially easier, our approach didn't change. And we never felt the need to lavishly celebrate

Valentine's Day, mainly because every day together was like a celebration. I sometimes thought to myself, 'If I drop down dead tomorrow, I am so grateful and fortunate to have experienced the most treasured of gifts – true love and happiness in my family life.' Everything was moving in the right direction, and when the time came, we had the longer term plan to retire to Italy, the South of France, or even settle back in Belgium.

However, from about 2009, a stealthy undercurrent began to stir the calmed sea that was our life when Winnie started to develop some symptoms attributed to early menopause, being only forty-three. She was often feeling drained, with more headaches and the unwelcome advent of hot flushes. This was coupled with a very busy and demanding new job, which meant that by the end of the working day and week, she was often mentally exhausted. Winnie's work ethic was so inflexibly strong, and she was unable to give herself a break or consider lowering her standards or her effort. Consequently, she worried that she was somehow losing herself, her spark and enthusiasm for life, and was very self-critical of her 'performance' as a wife and a mother, despite our regular and genuine assurances. It was painful for her to accept that her natural optimism had been compromised and diminished. Although we were reassured that the health effects she was experiencing were due to hormonal changes, Winnie had her family history of cancer at the back of her mind. Virtually all members on her dad's side had developed and not survived the disease, a permanent and patient shadow upon Winnie, whispering at her shoulder. However, we adapted and learned to manage the occasional frustrations and upset over time, while still being blissfully happy.

In August 2013, our summer holidays were spent in Belgium at her mum's lovely peaceful home, a haven that we had enjoyed for years. Winnie especially needed the break, as the stress from battling to maintain her standards had stretched her to the limit. Over a period of time, you get used to the changes, you cope together with difficulties, and the resulting situation becomes the norm. Winnie was not herself during the two weeks, struggling to relax and settle into a peaceful state of mind. On occasions, she showed less patience for things, snapped at her mum and me, was unpredictably tearful and a little clumsy – all things highly out of character. At other times, she was in a better place, so contented to meet up with all her close friends as we invariably did during our trips to Belgium. We didn't know it at the time of course, but this was Winnie's farewell to the people that she saw as part of her family. Sadly, most of them would not see her again.

Winnie was also sleeping more than usual, even for someone who loved her slumber. During one evening all cuddled up to watch a film on television, I remember looking at her sleeping during the movie, and seeing what I can only describe as pain etched on her face. She slept for most of the eight-hour drive back to Yorkshire. We had already decided that she had to go to the doctor again, that this had gone far enough, but still rationalising, as we had done for several years, that it was all due to the menopause.

I want to end this chapter by thanking Winnie Jane for the magic she brought to my life. This is why I love her, the way she made me feel… blessed, unique, precious, cherished for who I am, appreciated, respected, attractive, confident, utterly content and complete, excited, proud to be her husband, ready for anything, grateful, and wiser. She looked at me with such transparent love, opened my eyes to so much, broadened my horizons and opinions, learning and growing together. She was a dream but real all the same. When I took her hand, my heart ricocheted almost painfully in my chest with renewed delight, and she was always there for me, whatever the circumstances, hand in hand.

Chapter 2

Thirty-Five Days

Tuesday 13th August 2013. The alarm on my mobile phone sounded at 4.15am on the second day back at work, and I had a meeting in Amsterdam. Before leaving to drive to the airport, I leaned over the bed to gently kiss Winnie, who said she didn't feel well, and would be seeing the doctor that evening after work. *The image of her curled up in bed is forever in my mind's eye – the last time I saw her in our home.*

I felt relieved as I didn't want her to keep 'soldiering on' as she was prone to do. The day before, she said she couldn't remember how to work with one of the IT systems used regularly at work. Once I had landed safely, we had a brief chat, she seemed OK, we loved each other and I couldn't wait to return that evening. *The last conversation before our world collapsed.*

Stopping for lunch near the end of my meeting, I checked for messages on my phone, which had been switched to silent mode. I was confronted with a disconcerting number of missed calls. Shortly afterwards in a taxi, I listened in harrowing disbelief to the message from her boss that Winnie had been rushed to hospital with a suspected brain haemorrhage. Her friends at work had acted swiftly by recognising the signs and seriousness of Winnie's condition, and couldn't have done more for her. With the support of my friend and colleague John, I managed to catch an earlier flight back to the UK, albeit to a different airport from where I had flown that morning. During an interminable taxi journey to the hospital, I called Winnie's mum, fearful about what to say and for her reaction. In truth, I didn't yet know the full gravity of the situation. Finally arriving at the High Dependency Ward, being greeted by my mum and one of the doctors, I saw her. *We really are not prepared to see our loved ones in such a helpless condition.*

Winnie was semi-conscious, at least knowing I was there now. Much of the rest of that evening is lost to me, but I remember hearing that there was a bleeding on her brain, they were not yet sure of the cause as there was too much blood making the scan inconclusive, but it was not thought to be life-threatening. It had occurred on the left side of her brain, affecting the movement in her right arm and side, and her speech.

After collapsing into bed at midnight, a call two hours later woke me in confusion to this new reality. The surgeons needed to perform a fluid draining procedure to relieve the pressure on Winnie's brain, to which I gave my consent – anything to make her better. Twenty-four hours had passed that changed the direction of our lives, and nothing, apart from one thing (love…), would be the same thereafter.

Winnie's mum arrived shortly after, and the next days were an adrenalin driven blur, watching her every move for signs of improvement, and breaking the news to the family and friends in both countries, which was met with shock and incredulity. Some of our best friends, Jackie and Patrick, dropped everything in Belgium to be with her as quickly as possible. We were emboldened to see that Winnie was making progress, stabilising and showing more signs of consciousness and awareness in the tests the nurses carried out on an hourly basis. It was heartening to realise that she understood English, Dutch and French, although the very few words she did manage to articulate were mostly in English, even to her mum.

It appeared to me that all Winnie's worries and stresses had somehow melted away. Although she couldn't tell me in words, through her body language and mapping the expressions on the lovely face I knew so well, I understood that she felt a kind of relief, that the reason why she had been struggling so much to cope had finally revealed itself. She seemed lighter and far more carefree than before, and delighted in the kisses, hugs and hours of handholding that she received from all the loved ones who visited her. *My angel, free to soar again...* Indeed, she was so grateful to the nurses showing her kindness, that she wanted to reward them with a kiss too!

After little more than a week, she was well enough to move to another ward, and started the rehabilitation process. This focused mainly on her understanding of speech, and learning again how to use her right arm and hand. Although it was difficult for her to say much more than a few words, through her facial expressions and her attention to detail in choosing her clothes, we knew that her personality was not lost. Through the day while I worked, Nelly was at Winnie's side, caring for her daughter with such tenderness. Even though the doctors were surprised and pleased with Winnie's progress, at the back of my mind a nagging doubt resided, casting a shadow over the medical data and charts that suggested that Winnie was recovering. A visit from Sarah, one of her friends from work, provoked the doubt to come forth and confront me because, upon seeing Winnie, she could barely contain her upset and emotion. She could see through the shadow.

Despite these misgivings, a week later, Winnie was deemed to be well enough to progress to a specialist rehabilitation hospital. Our desperate optimism had for now won the battle, and Winnie was still determined to fight, shaking her fist and smiling in triumph when she learned of the transfer. My daughters, Nelly and I got to visit Winnie only once at this hospital. Her behaviour was more confused than before the move. Just before the end of visiting hours, Winnie was frustrated by not being able to quickly make us understand what she requested, which turned into an unwelcome guessing game. Eventually, we realised that she wanted to read her current book for the first time since she had fallen ill. *The last time I heard her voice.*

We walked reluctantly out of the ward, waving and blowing kisses, heartened by her desire to resume one of her passions, but with latent fear that the shadow remained.

Saturday 7th September 2013. The worst day of my life. Hope would be stolen and dismantled, never to be returned whole again. It started well, being another day, our positivity recharged. In an attempt to retain some normality to our lives, before visiting Winnie at hospital, the girls, a boyfriend and I played badminton at the local sports centre. Halfway through the game, my mobile rang with the news that Winnie had been rushed to the Accident & Emergency (A&E) back at the general hospital. She had suffered a seizure then another haemorrhage, probably caused by a brain tumour. *Was this really happening?* I knew it then, that this was not going away, that what had cast the shadow of doubt was finally looming into sinister full view.

The rest of the day was like living in the tragic film scenario that we have all seen and hoped would remain only fictional to us. Truly unbelievable that Nelly and I were two of its central characters. The surgeons were very clear about the stark options. If they performed an exploratory operation to discover the position and extent of the suspected tumour, there would be at least some brain damage. Should they do nothing, Winnie had no chance of survival in the coming twenty-four hours.

I was at the bottom of the abyss, further away from the light than I had ever been in this life, facing the enormity of the conse-quences ahead of us. But I didn't look away or hide, I didn't let the dreadful darkness consume me. Both Winnie and her mum needed me to be mentally strong and focused. I must thank my friend Ed, an A&E doctor at another hospital, who kept me anchored by calmly explaining things on the phone during the torturous few hours waiting for news. Winnie survived the operation we consented to that evening, and she was still in the fight.

The next days were spent in the Intensive Care Unit, where Winnie's breathing was sustained by a life support machine. Our sole aim was to give her any sort of comfort and love to let her know we were there. Playing her favourite music, a constant touch, a thousand kisses… she squeezed our hands to tell us she was still aware. There was a calmness and depth looking into her eyes that she knew it was serious, that this was her time.

The confirmation of what we all knew finally arrived. There was a very aggressive tumour in a place in the brain that was inoperable. No options remained, only a matter of time. The conversations with the doctors turned to when to start the procedures to let her go, and to organ donation. They agreed to my request to begin the day after because it was Friday 13th September. I took on the dreadful but important responsibility of informing everyone, as I was acutely aware that many people who loved her were constantly waiting for updates – she wasn't just my Winnie. The memory of breaking the news to the girls still hurts me now. They had mainly been protected from the worst of the reality, and to shatter their touching optimism felt so cruel.

With no escape from this devastating truth, and the imminent loss of my adored wife, before, I would have expected to completely fall apart. But no one knows how they'll react to such adversity until it becomes real. I experienced a state of calmness when the end was looming, somehow managing to stay relatively strong, clear thinking and composed. It may have been pure shock and disbelief, or a determined focus to ensure that Winnie did not suffer. Or maybe I knew instinctively that this was not the end, a deep seated, previously inaccessible knowledge and faith coming forward to guide me.

Winnie departed this life in her own time, on her own terms. The family from Belgium and England said their painful farewells. She still had an understanding of what was going on, there were tears in her eyes when her beloved stepdaughters kissed and held her, a terribly poignant and bittersweet experience to witness. For the final two nights in hospital, I was supported first by my brother Philip, and then by her uncle

Benoit, always like a second father to her, making sure that Winnie was never alone during her last hours. Just before, when I knew she was ready, I whispered in her ear,

'Winnie, your papa will be there for you, waiting to catch you.' *As if I was giving her back to Pierre, as he had done when I married his daughter.*

With no distress, she slipped peacefully away at 5am UK time on Monday 16th September 2013. Overwhelming sadness, but a sense of relief too, for she had clung on to life for much longer than anyone expected. The clock stopped for me at this moment, and has had to be reset for so many of Winnie's loved ones. *'Before and After'...The innermost, deepest part of my being will always remain in the 'Before', staying in that time when Winnie was alive in this world.*

I had never felt more love for her than when holding and caressing her hand in both of mine as she passed over. We had journeyed to the summit together. But on reaching what I believed was the peak, I was to learn that love endures and is able to climb to still higher places, sustained by a different quality of air.

Chapter 3

After: Survival

It only took a blink in life, after which I opened my eyes to a different domain. One that appeared to be powered by a dimmer, weaker light, drained of colour and vibrancy. The world is diminished by Winnie's absence. Individuals do make a difference, the magnitude only being fully understood when they're gone.

The pain was so bad because she and I were so good together. I woke to a nervous, unmoving, foreign presence in my stomach, carried the whole day, every day. My heart weighed heavy with grief, coupled with desolate emptiness. Yet, at the same time, overwhelming love completely filled and buoyed me. To be suddenly apart and remote from her, after the wonder of sharing and experiencing everything together, was suffocating and deeply disconcerting. Not that I had a death wish, but it felt like I absolutely should be there with Winnie, just as always. *All I wanted was to be by her side. Will there ever be another perfect day in my life, one without the contentment of just being with her?*

I started writing down my thoughts a few hours after she died. I needed an outlet, a way to make some kind of sense of it all. From that first day, I wrote directly to her, as if she would be receiving the worded messages and my thoughts. Apart from what was recorded, I have almost no recollection of how the first days, weeks and months were survived, how I arrived at where I am. Winnie had left an enormous hole in our lives, the void claiming all recognition of the aftermath. The brain's natural, merciful anaesthetic.

I have been fortunate by always being able to pick out 'silver linings' from virtually any situation. It was a true blessing that our family had those first three unforgettable weeks with Winnie after she fell ill to reaffirm how much she was loved. The emotional burden was eased knowing that I had no damaging regrets to haunt me. Nothing was left unsaid. So many people are not afforded this time and opportunity, so there was much to be grateful for, and it was a joy and privilege to have been her husband and best friend.

A few hours into this new world, at the hospital café, I took a picture on my phone, prompted by Winnie's mum. Looking back, I don't really know why I captured this image of my cup of cappuccino coffee topped with a chocolate heart. It was like any other of the servings that numerous people too had looked down upon already that morning in the café. Yet this gentle, unremarkable moment somehow signalled the beginning of a joyous and often incredible theme in our lives.

Soon, I'll tell the stories just as we experienced them. Taken alone, some may seem purely coincidental and easy to explain by those having doubts. But when all that has happened is viewed as a whole, coupled with the timing of many of the events, I believe these things are indeed connected, have meaning, and are real…

Everything, *every thing* about her is precious to me. Every kiss, every touch and laugh. The contents of her handbag, the clothes she was wearing the day when everything changed, the teacup she used at work, from trivial texts and emails to tender letters of love. And memories. They began as mortal enemies, each stabbing at my heart, ghosts trying to storm the fragile fortress of my composure. However, I knew there was to be no easy pathway through the searing hurt. The pain was best sought and confronted. The mental souvenirs would eventually become dear friends to celebrate and embrace, still alive, still real. The only unwelcome visitors were thoughts of the future, of things that we could be doing together, but never would. Thankfully I have mostly been able to repel such wounding imaginations, those chillingly, sickeningly devoid of comfort and healing.

Keeping perspective was a clear goal for me and my family, that there would be no self-pity from losing Winnie. *She absolutely could not tolerate people acting as victims.* She was the one who had lost most, and I ensure that we never forget that. It was important to adopt her attitude to this, which has helped to maintain a positive mindset.

The family came together to help to arrange the funeral, the Vicar visiting twice to discuss the service, to gain an impression of Winnie, and to give solace. In providing details for her eulogy, the Vicar revealed that he sensed I would be OK, even so few days after her passing. Two songs had to be chosen, one to accompany the mourners filing into the service, the other to bid them farewell. I settled on the choice for the latter almost immediately – *Walk the Road (together)* by Kate Rusby. However, the first one, the scene setter, proved to be a far harder challenge to convey the right balance of a positive message and being appropriate for the day. Sitting at my home office desk upstairs in the house, I set about the long list of selected 'possibles'. Downstairs, music was playing, one of Winnie's playlists of over fifty songs, filling the house with sounds that made her happy. It was a relatively easy task to eliminate many of the songs, since the purpose was now clearer to me. I came upon *Don't Dream It's Over* by Neil Finn, a beautiful live acoustic version with some crowd noise and applause. We both loved the song, but I rejected it after brief reflection, simultaneously, sadly putting a line through the title on the page. At that very same moment, our home breathed out a new song from the playlist. 'Don't dream it's over,' it sang. Laughing through fresh tears, I immediately understood and accepted the message. The choice had been made.

This was the first suggestion of a sign. I didn't care if this was just a delicious and benevolent coincidence or not. It seemed right, with the perfect timing and the perceived meaning in the words of the title…

Family and friends gathered from far and wide to remember

23

Winnie. She would be proud how we held ourselves together on this day, still dazed, trying to grasp that it was actually happening. In keeping with Winnie's generosity and thoughtfulness, I wanted to do something lasting for the women closest to her, so I selected a piece of her jewellery for each of them to keep. These little things can have great individual meaning.

During the next three weeks, I made some significant discoveries, coming across Winnie's forgotten books on spirituality, karma and the afterlife. *My instinct told me immediately, 'She wants me to read these books, so I had better get on with it.'* In a sketchbook of hers, a coloured drawing of a heart, and an attractive monochrome depiction of her name (Figure 1) were unearthed.

Both were given prominent positions in the kitchen, the centre of our home. However, this would not be the last resting place of 'her name picture', to be explained later. Finally during this period, another item came into my view. Just by the catflap built into the wall of the house, having no idea how it got there, sat a heart that had been attached to Winnie's key ring. *Was I supposed to find all these things?*

After starting to read some of the revelations in Winnie's books, it seemed the natural next step for me to contact a locally recommended medium, albeit only six weeks after Winnie had passed over. It's true that I already believed in life after death, but intuition told me that this would help and possibly provide further insight.

First visit to the medium

The medium said she would simply transmit what the spirits passed on to her, without knowing if it made sense to me. I had given no prior details about me or my situation, apart from the fact that my wife had passed away, and no further information was requested.

Medium: There is an older man making contact. Would your wife have someone who'd passed away who she would want to rejoin with?

Me: Yes, her dad.

Medium: He's pointing to his chest and coughing [Pierre died of lung cancer].

Medium: There is something about a rose [At the funeral, my mum wrote, 'Winnie, a beautiful rose of Belgium and England.'] and there is a female presence here now. I'm getting Australia. [Winnie and I had a long-term plan to visit my family and some friends in the next few years.] She says that you have to go there, it's easier for you now with the girls. [Winnie seemed to know that financially this would no longer be a problem.]

Medium: I'm now getting something about a boy. No it's twins actually. [Winnie was godmother to five year old twins. They had just visited her in hospital, and had brought a card with their drawings, which she had loved.]

Medium: You have something to do with Scotland or the North.

Me: Not really.

Medium: Or it could be the Lakes.

Me: What made you change to the Lakes?

Medium: Winnie showed me an image of beautiful lakes and scenery. [In June, we had spent a wonderful time in the Lake District for our 8th wedding anniversary, and had been planning to return with her mum and uncle in September.]

Medium: I can tell that she was a very intelligent and stable person, with a good career and a very happy life. She was kind and gentle but assertive, not afraid to say things that needed to be said. She says that your relationship was very solid, close and loving.

At this point, the medium transmitted details about Winnie's illness, and started to feel some physical effects.

Medium: Right now, I'm feeling sick and dizzy in my head. Everyone was so shocked how suddenly it all happened and how serious it was. It was only about four weeks. She had not been feeling well for some time, with headaches etc, but she says that she didn't want to use painkillers because she doesn't believe in that [this was exactly her attitude to taking pills, and what she would say]. You went to see the specialists and they said that Winnie had nothing to lose – if they did nothing, she would die, and if they operated then at least they'd have a chance to see what was possible.

Then the medium described how she was feeling.

Medium: It feels like a big block of concrete on top of my head. It all started at one side of the head, then a little at the front then more at the back. I can feel that Winnie was a spiritual person, and she says she had books on the subject. She repeated that we must go to Australia twice more, just so I got the message!

Medium: There is another female now present with Winnie and her dad. She is also pointing to her chest and says that this is what caused her to pass away [I instantly thought of one of Winnie's best friends who had died of breast cancer some years earlier].

The medium then enquired if anything unusual had been happening at home, like with electrical appliances, lights being switched on and off, or the feeling of a gentle touch on the arm or face. I replied no, to which she advised me to be ready for, and open to, this sort of occurrence. *This proved to be prophetic.*

I sat in my car after emerging from this meeting with a feeling of complete, calm elation. The results were more than I could have hoped for, the medium passing on this personal information of such accurate detail that she could not possibly have known. This was consistent with other accounts that I read, in which much of the first reading focuses on how the person died, and the receiver of the messages is left in no doubt about their authenticity.

The very next morning after this momentous event, I was making breakfast, and automatically took a towel to mop up the condensation that always formed on the main window in the living room at that time of year. Striding over to wipe the pane, I was halted in momentary confusion by what I saw on the window, first thinking it was a trick of the light. The water usually appeared as an opaque sheet covering most of the window. But this time, the vapour had formed a distinct heart (Figure 2) that I had the good fortune to notice. The significance

of the timing of this was not lost on me, and I quickly captured the image on my phone. *This was the first time that I had any conscious idea that maybe Winnie had sent me a sign, or indeed had the ability to do so. You cannot imagine the sheer joy I felt, in light of what had just happened at the medium's the day before, when I realised what I was looking at, and that she was trying to 'talk' to me.*

I had recently experienced a dream of such convincing reality that the clarity remains, not spirited away by time, as happens in most normal instances. With no element of fantasy, we met in a subconscious world, sat on a bed and just cried together. No words were needed or uttered. We knew all too well what had happened to us. This was a powerful enough 'happening', and other dreams would later confer profound meaning, but the heart on the window was different in that an image of it could be shared.

Throughout those first hard months of intense emotion after losing Winnie, there was so much concern and support from family and friends, kindness that will never be forgotten. It was when recounting the visit to the medium and the heart on the window that I learned that they too had amazing and sometimes beautiful, inexplicable stories to tell, so I began to keep track of the experiences in one of her old notebooks.

When Winnie suffered the first haemorrhage, I had waited until the day after to break the news. I was astonished with the revelation that in Belgium one of our friends, Carolien, had repeatedly shouted out in her panicked sleep, 'They're putting something in my head!' This turned out to be at the same time in the middle of the night when the surgeons had fitted a stent to drain the fluid on Winnie's brain. *It was a struggle to take in this news, to comprehend the implications of it.*

Then on the night before the funeral, some Belgian friends were staying in a local hotel. Nadia was woken by light in the room; then seeing that the whole blank TV screen was lit white nudged her husband Ronald to get up to switch it off. He found to their confusion that it was already off! It transpired that the same event had also happened twice at Carolien and Sven's house recently when I shared this story.

A short while after Winnie had passed over, two separate couples close to us had lost a piece of jewellery of important significance to them, causing much upset and regret. One friend was so distraught that she took the loss to be an ominous sign that their marriage was in jeopardy. On both occasions, after accepting defeat, having searched everywhere without success, they were reunited with their elusive prizes in the most obvious and visible places; one on the kitchen top next to the kettle, the other in what appeared to be a cleared space in a drawer they used daily for keys, etc. Both couples said they instantly and instinctively thought of Winnie, wondering if she could have somehow played a part in these discoveries. *All I know is that it was a certain, fundamental part of Winnie's character that she would want to help her loved ones in any way possible, family and friends alike. What a wonderful thought that these could have been two examples of this.*

Winnie's ashes are buried at the local cemetery, ten minutes' walk from the house. I had been feeling low and emotionally fragile at the time, and hated the stark reminder of reality visiting this place, but I made the undertaking to place fresh flowers there regularly. After bending down to do this, while saying a few strained words to my dear departed, I stood up wearily to look down on the blooms. I was sure that what I saw was distorted by the thick tears in my eyes. But no, upon the shiny black marble of the small commemorative gravestone (the plaque with her details still had to be fitted) again a clear heart shape presented itself (Figure 3). I snapped out of my sombre mood,

intrigued to find out what the shape was made from, after taking a photo of course. Simple water. *The message appeared to be that she felt my pain and wanted to heal.*

Winnie liked nothing better than to be in her kitchen, so it was fitting that, when we started noticing objects move, they would mostly happen in her favourite place at home. My oldest daughter, Gabrielle, was at the breakfast bar doing her French homework, while I was washing up. She alerted me to one of the cups on the mug tree that was directly in front of her eyeline from where she was working. It was swaying gently whilst all the others were completely still. Our smiles lit up with recognition when I assured her that I had not disrupted the mug tree. And some months later, alone in the kitchen, Gabrielle called me in an excited panic while I was driving. This time, all the mugs hung on the tree were swinging more quickly, again without having been touched.

The girls had always been allowed to borrow any of Winnie's things on condition that they looked after them. She had always taken such pleasure and pride in caring for her clothes and footwear, and I wanted to continue this 'tradition'. Gabrielle wore Winnie's favourite pair of black leather gloves on Christmas Day, and that night remembered to carefully place them together on the table in her bedroom. She had also sent a little prayer for a sign from her stepmum on this special day, and woke to find that overnight one of the gloves had separated from the other by a distance of around a metre.

On another occasion, Gabrielle told me with wide eyes that Winnie's name picture (Figure 1) had moved in front of her, and then fallen down on to the kitchen work surface. All the doors and windows were closed, so we knew it was not caused by a sudden draft. A few days afterwards, the same happened before my own eyes. Having risen alone to make breakfast, starting with a cup of tea, I made my way towards the kettle. As I reached for it, my peripheral vision picked up a movement reflected in the glossy grey paint of a wall cupboard. *My mind registered it to be a shadow, but what had cast it from behind me?* A split second after, I first heard, and then looked on in amazement: the paper with her name on it had slid softly down from where it had been lodged moments before. *It happened again more than a year later, on the occasion of the early morning of her birthday to find the paper displaced again, a heartening gift of immeasurable value.*

With the unfolding of all these different events, there was of course much animated discussion among family and friends, most of whom had never seen or heard anything like it. One of our very best friends in Belgium was keen to understand and join the 'club' of those that had received or perceived a sign. However, after listening avidly, he asked an understandable question: 'But how?' I could only reply that there is no answer to that, it just 'is'. *Even in the face of a growing number of wondrous occurrences, I realised and respected that for various reasons some are not so open to such ideas without absolute proof, and so are unable to take that mental leap of faith. Perhaps a better question would have been 'Why?', for which I could have at least attempted an answer. Winnie was a gifted communicator on a very personal level, who dearly loved her family and friends, and loved to show it...*

On the other hand, my mum had always been a believer. And she had been extremely close to her daughter-in-law, forging a beautiful bond during the early years when times were difficult. All the discussion about signs suddenly unlocked a recent memory that may never have been freed, happening on the day that Winnie died. We had all sensed that Monday 16th September would be the last day. Before sunrise, thought to be at around 5am (the time of passing), Mum was drifting in and out of fitful sleep, anticipating the dreaded call, when she was shocked to remember being nudged by someone getting into bed beside her! She duly made space without thinking, then recollection faltered after that, but she was certain it was not my dad, who was tucked up in his own bed. *As stunned as we were happy, this was another example of an experience that left us shaking our heads in wonder and contemplation of what may be going on in our midst, usually without awareness.*

In contrast to the more physical signs that her older sister had seen, my daughter Francesca's perception of Winnie's presence was on a more subtle, instinctive level. One day, on our way out of the house, she had the strong feeling that someone passed her en route to the garage. She had thought it was one of us, but Gabrielle and I were already seated in the car, ready to leave. Another time, she entered the kitchen in darkness and instantly sensed a shape in the corner by the main photograph of Winnie. Around the same period, one evening some weeks after her passing, I switched the kitchen light on and walked the few paces to one of the units. Something passed across me at chest height from left to right moving quite quickly, almost as if I had caused surprise or disturbance. My first simultaneous thought, trying to process it into something recognisable, was that it must have been a piece of agglomerated dust that you often see collecting on hard floors. All happening in the space of less than two seconds, I looked down to the right of the kitchen unit to check if my rational assumption was correct, but there was nothing there. It was then that I could 'rewind' and review what I had actually seen. I can only describe it as a translucent, golden brown wispy ribbon, unlike anything I have beheld in my life. *Intuition told me that it must have been something to do with my wife, whose 'spirit' seemed to be busy startling us with an array of dumbfounding episodes.*

The first months after Winnie's death had been understandably bleak for Nelly. The sorrow of losing not just her husband, but now her only daughter was a cruel burden to bear. Winnie had been a pillar of strength for her ever since Pierre's passing, so even I could hardly imagine the hell that poor Nelly was going through. We spoke on most days, the two people who best understood each other's loss, and were able to express it. It was so important for her to know that she still had her English family, that this wouldn't change, and staying in regular contact provided some small semblance of continuity since the tragedy. In addition, I realised very quickly that for Nelly to find some peace in the longer term, my vital task was to gently introduce the idea of Winnie's spirit living on. It had to be done with sensitivity and patience though, since I knew Nelly was unlikely to have seriously contemplated such a notion before, and didn't want to cause her yet more upset.

In my less than perfect Dutch, I started to describe some of the experiences, and asked a friend to translate the transcript of my first visit to the medium for her. The combination of these new insights, and many talks with a particularly close friend in Belgium (who coincidentally, or perhaps tellingly, also happens to be English!) allowed Nelly to open up, and begin to set her grief free. Slowly, her mainly negative mindset, fuelled by uplifting new belief, was migrating from the cold to warmer climes. Before, she had been tormented by thoughts that could only bring more pain. The truth is that the simple, recurring question 'Why Winnie?' could have caused damage to Nelly for the rest of her life. What a relief, then, that not only did she embrace these spiritual ideas, but soon after started to receive her own signs as she opened up to them.

They seemed to begin in a manner for her to take notice, 'easy' communications for her to pick up, in a sense. The first suggestion of one happened on the day before Winnie's birthday, little more than three months since her death. Nelly had gone into the local village for some shopping. On her return, she entered to hear music coming from somewhere in the house. This unnerved her as she was meticulous in turning everything off before leaving. In the living room, she found the iPod playing, though it was unfortunate she neglected to take note of the song, but her composure had been momentarily shaken. A few days later, while dusting in the same room, the television suddenly came on, without any intervention from Nelly.

In the eight years since Pierre's passing, her occasional dreams about him had sadly always left a feeling of regret and pessimism. However, this time similar to my own experience, she had an incredibly vivid dream about her husband, in which he was ecstatic to be with her, offering comfort and support as he had before. *Like a thick, heavy door had been found and opened, and at long last she was now ready to move to a higher level of understanding.*

The next story is perhaps my favourite, and for which Nelly and I have absolutely no plausible explanation. So I'm just going to tell it how it happened. We were talking about the prospect of her imminent visit to a medium in Belgium, taking those next steps, and I remember saying, 'De deur is nu open' ('the door is open now'). She only informed me afterwards, but during the call, she heard a kind of soft clinking in the room, but, concentrating on our conversation, absent-mindedly thought it was only one of her two cats. She rose once the call finished, and, being keenly house proud, immediately noticed the doors of a cabinet were ajar. Every good Belgian living room needs a large cabinet to house the multitude of different glasses designed for each beer, the country's crown jewels. Conspicuously on the floor in front of the open doors was placed a distinctive glass, but not just any glass. It was the one used for the beer named 'Palm'... Winnie's favourite! There was little question that Nelly could have simply forgotten to tidy the glass away, since she was teetotal and alone, and in any case, the glasses were there only for the benefit of visiting family and friends. *A healing gift of a sign to Nelly, perhaps for the first time conveying Winnie's character, somehow as if we were working together to encourage her 'ma'ke' (mum) to take the next steps.*

A short time later, Nelly, together with one of Winnie's best friends, Gerda, attended a reading with a medium, the results of which had the desired effect on her whole outlook. The lady she saw was a very gifted psychic, able to convey personalities of those passed over, giving many personal details, and relaying the words she heard using the exact type of language that her husband and daughter would have used. Nelly learned that the two of them were happy and well together, and would be helping us all to soothe our pain. At one point, Nelly felt a distinctive tingling on her fingertips and her arm, which she was told signified their presence. The medium saw Winnie trace a large heart around an image of herself and I, declaring, 'This is the love of my life,' and wanted me to know that she would watch over the girls and help as much as she could. *Still caring, and committed to her family...*

She also declared her dearest wish was for me to find happiness. Winnie's mum gained relief beyond measure from this encounter, her whole demeanour softening almost instantly. Much to my own relief, it was evident she had turned the corner, and was heading towards light and hope instead of the continual dead end of darkness and despair.

In a separate reading during the same evening, Gerda was also in contact with Winnie, requesting some advice as she'd always done in the past, this time about her problematic job situation. She was revealingly counselled: 'not to focus so much on the job, work and things needing to be done, thus avoiding mistakes she had made. Start enjoying your personal life more, because that's far more important.'

Meanwhile, there were yet more stories to be told back in England. My oldest brother had listened in wonderment to all the stories of the signs. Then just a week later, while half asleep alone at home, he was roused to a stunned wakefulness by his hair being ruffled, almost teasingly. Elsewhere, a good friend had developed some worrying health symptoms, and was due to receive the test results that day. Driving to work, his wife was in a distressed state in anticipation of bad news, when something happened that boosted her resolve and faith that her husband was going to be fine. On the car radio during that journey, the song *Don't Dream It's Over* played, all our friends and family being aware of the meaning this song had. And happily, our friend's results were not as serious as had been feared. *How the positive energy generated and disseminated by such stories of love and kindness have helped us to look to the horizon with a smile...*

I must confess that my household cleaning standards were never very high at the best of times, and especially in my tiny home office. This neglect often resulted in an impatient reminder from Winnie, head shaking in mild admonishment, as the rest of our home gleamed in comparison, but she knew that I just didn't notice like she did. Since Winnie's passing, it's safe to say that my office had descended into an even worse state than before. One day, working intently at my desk, I looked down at my laptop keyboard to find a small clump of dust. Being in the middle of something that commanded my full attention, I automatically brushed away the dust without thinking. A couple of hours later, another clump of dust had found its way on to my keyboard again! This time, I woke up to this unusual occurrence, observing the dust and instinctively looking around behind me before my gaze was drawn down to the skirting boards. I truly had not appreciated how much of the stuff had collected there, and bursting into action, my office was soon back in acceptable condition.

The humour in this sign really made me smile, appearing to be a reminder from Winnie, just as before, to get on with cleaning that bloody office up!

A few weeks on, a related event, again full of humour, further bolstered the view that something remarkable was afoot. A good friend and my twin godsons had stayed the night, and after brunch, I quickly tidied the clean bowls and plates on to the kitchen cabinet, ready to put away shortly. In the meantime, with much pleasure, I recounted the story of the dust in the office, then on my return to the kitchen, the revelation... settled proudly in the centre of the stacked bowls was a clump of dust, just willing to be noticed! *My instant thought was that she's saying, 'You're right, love, you got the message, and it was me.'*

Around the same period, some good friends were due to come over for dinner one Saturday evening, and I had to shop for a few last minute items, including some potato crisps. Deciding on a particular flavour, I had to rummage to the back of the shelf to find the last remaining packet. Then back at the house, having drinks before dinner, I reached for a crisp, pulling one out that was a perfect heart shape, making us gasp, given the background to what had ensued lately.

Meeting up with the same friends on the first of Winnie's birthdays without her, two of us were sat having coffee, just talking about everyday matters. A few seconds after I made a mental note to remain open and alert to any kind of sign from her on this special day, something actually did happen. My shin and knee were resting against a wooden stool, which suddenly jolted with what felt like an unmistakably intentional movement, but not made by myself. Both the scraping noise and the abrupt push against my leg surprised me, rapidly snapping my head around, fully expecting to find that someone, a child most probably, had just clipped the stool in passing. There was absolutely no person (nor dog) to be seen in the vicinity. *I like to think that she was giving me a little nudge, a playful reminder.*

Whilst the marvel of the tender, reassuring messages that suggested Winnie's presence prevented me from sinking into perpetual sorrow, there were of course countless grim moments. Many people confided that they had no conception of how it felt to be without someone so loved and fundamental to your life, as Winnie had been for me. So I tried to put it into words a year after her passing... 'Every day in a boat, rowing alone on the open sea, sometimes placid, perhaps even a passing ray of sunshine, otherwise stormy, unpredictable, terrifying. Daring not to look ahead over the silent, endless, empty expanse of ocean. Dull numbness. Nights are the islands, the safe havens reached at the end of each day. The chance to meet her, crossing a bridge, away from the sea, from the waking day and the reality.

Every day hurts, a mental struggle, a battle on the waves, rowing to reach the safety and solace of my island, gaining strength and resolve to begin tomorrow's journey afresh. Neither lost, nor searching for other lands, I seek but one destination, my island. As ever, she is my lighthouse, my guide, leading me to calmer waters and to sunshine.'

It's true that I have started to settle into the new situation, learning to cope without her. However, underpinned by the belief that she is still with me in spirit, I reject the whole idea of 'moving on', that which somehow implies things are better left behind and forgotten. Time has a lesser meaning to me now. Two weeks, two years, it has no bearing, and is no practical measure of how I should be feeling. While time may well erode the sharp edges of emotional pain and loss, the mountainous longing is impervious and unchanging. The sadness and missing of her is my constant companion, solid and unyielding, yet a cavernous space left by her. Faithfully, I carry it, residing in the centre of my chest, a partner for my heart. But the missing is not a completely empty, negative space. We're somehow inseparable. We are still connected.

Of all the myriad of things cherished about Winnie, the joy of sharing with her is yearned the most. We always knew that whatever befell us, we lived it together as one, giving everything we had to each another, sharing in the laughter and the lament, our dreams and fears. *So, what an offering of potent, restorative love, to gain the trust that we are never alone moving through the sunshine and shadow of our lives.*

Thankfully, the blessing of such a close relationship with my daughters has kept me positive and focused on their needs, and my role as their dad. Every tentative step forward has been taken together, and I really could not be any prouder of them for their courage and maturity in the face of our family tragedy.

Needing to escape on a bike ride one Sunday morning, I deliberated for a few minutes on which route to take, eventually choosing one that leads to a peaceful place in woodland by a canal. On arrival at my favoured spot by the banks of the canal, failing to contain my composure a second longer, I whispered to Winnie that I liked to come to this place to talk to her, to feel closer. The shortest instant after voicing those tearful words, two pristine white swans glided silently into view. Immediately remembering them to be one of the few species to have a sole partner for life, I was entranced by their natural elegance and unity. They stayed for a couple of minutes, seemingly observing me, before continuing towards the January sun, settled low above the tranquil water.

A moment of beauty and grace, a symbol of togetherness, a reminder that there still are wonders in this world, all things that reminded me of her. But in my eyes, nothing so lovely...

Chapter 4

After: Living in Two Worlds

With all that I'd seen, sensed and heard from others up to this point, an impatient eagerness drove me to research more into the related subjects. It somehow brought me nearer to Winnie. I thirsted to understand and imagine what 'existence' was like for her now. There was no doubt in my faithful inner voice, urging me that this was the right thing to do, what I must do. On more than a few occasions, a book would be recommended by someone I shared some of the experiences with, which further increased my learning. *Leading me to conclude that when we adopt a more open attitude to people who cross our paths, new understanding and insight can be gained, and unexpected, but somehow pertinent connections made. I'd love to think that Winnie's book could contribute positively in this way.*

I was beginning to see, not merely look. The signs I had received were never searched for, they just seemed to be in my path, there to be found. The studying and deep reflection combined to transport me effortlessly to a relaxed, almost hypnotic state when I wanted. *Was this what Winnie meant by reaching a higher level of consciousness?*

It felt like the right time to have a second reading with the medium, and the first opportunity for my daughters to accompany me. Although the experiences were perhaps less overwhelming than the first time, one small but astounding detail emerged that I still think of every day, to be explained shortly.

As before, the medium passed on random information of no meaning to her, in sharp contrast to us. Winnie said I was surprising myself how I was managing, becoming mentally stronger, 'walking through life, not running'. *I appreciated the words she used, more elegantly than I could have described how I was surviving.*

The medium said that Winnie was pointing to her neck to signify jewellery (I had been wearing her wedding ring on a leather necklace, but shortly before it had broken so I wasn't wearing it presently).

Images of mountains were described, the medium thinking of the Alps in Switzerland, a country where I often worked, and was due to visit three weeks later. It appeared that she also knew I was exercising a lot. True enough, I found that cycling and working out at the gym were helping me physically and mentally.

Francesca asked if the medium could actually see Winnie, and on hearing an affirmative answer, the girls were instructed to place a hand in a space about 30 cm above the table between them to feel that the air there was icy cold. *I'd heard about similar descriptions of spirits, and was touched to contemplate that this could be a very special kind of physical connection with her.* The medium then shared intimate details about their characters and what was going on in their lives. *Just as she had promised during Nelly's medium reading in Belgium, Winnie was watching over her girls.*

I was intrigued to be informed that there was another spirit present, with whom the medium made no contact, only that it was a very gentle older woman. *Something told me that it was my maternal grandma, with whom I had been very close, and who had played a major part in my childhood.*

Now to the event that strengthened my own belief that communication can exist and operate on other, more advanced levels. Very soon after Winnie passed away, I wrote in her notebook that our little greengage tree in the front garden was always going to be special to me. While Winnie was in hospital, in fact making progress at the time, the tree began to bear fruit for the very first season. So every day I picked her a ripe plum (and a Belgian chocolate) as a treat. I'll always remember with warming affection her delighted expression with the dawning realisation that the plum I initially awarded had come from our own tree, as if a memory of home was triggered. She then grabbed it from my hand with startling agility, and devoured it in one quick action. And now, seven months later at the reading, the medium said, 'She's showing both of you planting a small tree.'

In fact, three or four years earlier, that is exactly what we had done, hoping for healthy growth, a future offering of the tree's natural gifts, an indication of maturing life.

I am unable to properly describe my epiphany, the revelation of this moment. It led me to think of roots, origins deep beneath our superficial layers, beyond what we can only see. However impossible it may seem, it was like she knew my thoughts and feelings, the significance of our little greengage tree, and chose to present this past event to communicate this to me. And maybe part of the plan was for me to be sharing this now with you.

For years, we had spent Easter in Belgium with Nelly, and it was important to maintain that tradition after Winnie's passing. She was everywhere in the house, the recollections so vivid and raw, bringing comfort or yearning at any moment. One early evening during our stay, I was on my way to the bathroom when I had the compulsion to say to myself out loud, 'OK, what have you got for me now, Winnie?' Being drawn to look out of the window, I relaxed and took in what there was to observe. After a couple of minutes, I focused on a crane in the near distance, and in particular the shape of its hook block.

Of course, the heart shape of the block was there for all to see at any time. But how enchanting, the feeling that I had been guided to seek it out.

Around six months later, in our bedroom exercising, a strong instinct arrived unexpectedly for me to turn on the lamp on a set of drawers. The idea just popped into my thoughts, like a radio channel being switched by surprise, by someone else. This lamp was in fact very rarely used, and at that moment there was

absolutely no reason to do so. Shrugging my shoulders, but still following my intuition, as soon as the light beamed out, I was completely taken aback by the projected result (Figure 4) caused by the random arrangement of books and papers stacked on the drawers, perhaps tellingly next to a small but proud Belgian flag. *Just as she did in life, it was as if Winnie was displaying her love, opening my eyes, almost challenging me to gain greater awareness and understanding. I'm following her lead...*

She does know my thoughts and feelings. Sharing in our memories, reliving them with me, linked by invisible threads. Our paths are bound, my hand still in hers.

Dreams were rich in detail, and overwhelming. Holding a hand, I recognised it to be hers, flexing my grip, confirming the familiarity, the smoothness and texture of her skin. Never before had I experienced such a physical sensation in that blissful merging of wake and sleep, where two streams fuse together and flow into the same river. *A dream, but real all the same. To me, memories and images experienced in this state, recalled through the mind's eye, appeared every bit as authentic as those lived and remembered in the waking world.*

I had another shuddering mindful dream in which I was with Winnie on the top of a small hill in summertime. We didn't talk but she showed a kind of handheld board for me to read: 'Wonderful,' it said. Then we travelled down the hill together, on the tracks created through the crops in the field, still able to remember even now the exact colour of the green leafed plants. This encounter on its own already had a healing effect on me, and for the next few weeks when riding my bike in the forest near our home, I sought to relive this somehow familiar scene.

One day, like a mental matching process was going on, while riding I had the sudden recognition of the place where we'd met in the dream, so I hastily parked my bike against a tree in the forest to walk back for a better look. Two small steps later, a considerable thud sounded behind me. Thinking with annoyance that my bike had fallen down, I turned around, astonished to see that a grey squirrel had jumped down from high up to land right beside my upright bike. Had I not moved a second before, it would have landed on top of me! At the time I thought, 'What's going on? Squirrels usually run the other way from people.' It proceeded to climb another tree, settling on a low branch, just watching me for a couple of minutes, while I returned the gaze in fascination. I pondered if the timing of this was significant: this unusual happening coming straight after thinking I recognised the place in my dream. And of course, I took a photo, really just to mark the event rather than capturing something concrete that I had seen. Zooming into this image some days later, I was enthused to find that a few heart shapes were visible, caused by the light shining through the tree canopy. Though, to be honest, my rational, logical voice told me this was but a charming coincidence, probably not uncommon when similar forest photos are observed in close detail. However, a later finding led me to reconsider this initial assumption. Two years before, Winnie and I selected a print of a work by the Belgian artist Magritte to hang in the hallway of our house. It's called *L'Empire des Lumieres (The*

Empire of Lights). This alluring painting is unusual because it cleverly depicts blue sky in daylight, whilst the rest of the scene appears to be at night. It serves me well as a constant, almost reassuring reminder of a subtle recurring theme – that life is fundamentally about the twin contrast of light and dark, of cyclic joy and sorrow. Then a few weeks after taking the photo of the forest, the idea surfaced to scrutinise the painting, revealing something fortifying, something enlightening. In the print, tiny yet distinct heart shapes are painted into the trees. Just as in the forest photo I took. *Like an inner compass had naturally steered me along a pathway to this affirmative point of enigmatic symmetry. No matter which way you turn, love and compassion are there to be found, present, always...*

My belief in the integrity of these messages was further illuminated when returning to Winnie's name picture (Figure 1) found together with the coloured heart in her sketchbook. Years before, she had drawn a shining sun, waves of peaks and troughs, and circles shaded light and dark. All now symbols of enormous value and intense meaning to me that I hadn't noticed until gaining these further insights. Then, almost two and half years after her passing, in a wedding photo (Figure 5) that had been looked at hundreds of times, I saw something new, familiar and profound. Our joined hands perfectly intersect the balanced light and dark background, bound together for the challenges ahead. *Everything seems connected. And what of destiny?*

Bittersweet. For some reason, these words always had a mysterious quality for me in the back of my mind, a clouded, uncomprehending attraction to the concept. Without any doubt, I now have clarity of the meaning, the devastation, the desolation of losing her, married to intense, pure and lasting feelings of love. They somehow belong together.

First anniversaries of notable dates were perhaps less distressing than I'd imagined they would be. Of course, it was impossible to prevent thoughts of these happy days of the past, and what we might be doing now... on the 4th of June, our wedding date, I was able to focus on this as one of the very best days of my life, a flood of touching details, so clear and vibrant. But in the end, it was just another day without her.

Especially during the first year, I often lit a tea light candle, and placed it in the corner of the living room close to where Winnie had always sat. This humble, pure light conveyed a reassuring presence, a constant symbolic remembrance of her. I sometimes watched our wedding video, the joy of seeing her so happy and carefree outweighing the still raw grief. On one occasion, turning back to smile at her candle behind me during

an emotional moment, I was captivated by the beautiful shape the flame had formed (Figure 6).

In discussion with my cousin Elaine, we had the idea to ask one of her friends, Elizabeth, to prepare a birth chart reading (horoscope) for Winnie, which basically plots the position of the planets, including the Sun, the Moon and the zodiac signs in the sky at the exact moment and place of a person's birth. In Greek, one interpretation of the word horoscope means 'watching from a high place'. This was quite an unusual request for a deceased person, but I explained my quest to acquire deeper insight into this 'unknown' part of my wife, and what her main purpose in this life was. *The more I know, the closer I am to her...*

Elizabeth is an experienced astrologer who has worked on birth chart readings for a number of years, the real skill being the interpretation of the chart of the person in question. It was an intriguing added bonus that she also has developing mediumistic ability. She and Winnie had never met, and my cousin had given no details of her life. However, in the weeks up to the visit, I learned that Elizabeth had formed a connection with Winnie, sensing her presence, and the love for her family. During the talk, when Elizabeth or I said something that Winnie particularly agreed with, either she felt a tingling on her face or arm, or she heard Winnie's affirmation. This happened when explaining how we were so in tune as a couple, happy that everyone had felt that about us.

Elizabeth interpreted Winnie to be an old, advanced spirit from her chart, characteristics, and her capability to communicate with us, especially being able to move objects. Elizabeth remarked what a pleasant person Winnie seems to be in spirit: sensitive, having innate wisdom, generous, giving, and very well balanced. She was loyal, with principles, good with numbers and practical with her hands, but also creative, and with much mental strength and determination. A natural communicator, accomplished in many things, and could have excelled in many different careers. People looked up to her for the wise, able and good person she was.

Family and relationships were the key theme of this life. She had a very happy and stable childhood, with some discipline but given the freedom to think for herself and make her own way. Elizabeth could sense that she was very close to both her parents.

The relationship with children was very important. Somehow, Elizabeth could sense in the chart there had been some difficulty here. As she said this, Elizabeth heard Winnie in her mind saying, 'I love the girls just like they are my own.'

Intimacy and connection with her partners was another strong theme, and her chart suggested she would marry someone from a different land (that's me!!). Elizabeth could detect shyness behind the obvious aptitude for communication with others, and not knowing beforehand, predicted that Winnie had a job in sales or promotion of some sort, which is correct. An unusual feature called the Grand Cross or Square dominated Winnie's chart. This can signify a huge challenge in a person's life, sometimes one that cannot be overcome. (When Elizabeth had written about this in a previous email to me, she heard in her mind the words 'but I was a fighter' from Winnie.)

Elizabeth saw nothing adverse in her chart, concluding this rare feature likely indicated the difficult, shocking death of someone so dear and important to her loved ones. In addition, the Grand Cross/Square can signify an exceptionally special person. All who knew her would acknowledge this to be true.

The only slightly negative aspects of her chart were in fact consequences of some of Winnie's strongest traits. Her mental determination and refusal to lower her high standards in every-thing she did caused some tension in her life, but this was simply part of her character.

Something tells me these qualities of hers will be needed to inspire me to ensure this book fulfils its purpose. It was astounding how accurate the interpretation of Winnie's birth chart had been. Although having no idea or understanding how she accomplished this, I am very grateful to Elizabeth for contributing important elements, adding depth and dimension from another source, to the overall picture that was emerging.

Meanwhile, one of my best friends from childhood was eager to let me know they had witnessed another 'Winnie moment' as he put it. He had stacked some plastic cups on a table nearby, while he and his youngest daughter sat at the computer together.

The moment they began looking at photos of Winnie, the cups toppled over for no obvious reason, maintaining there was no gust of wind nor anything else unusual that may have caused it.

I'm afraid to confess that another rather lazy housekeeping bad habit had developed since my wife was no longer around 'to keep me on my toes'. But I'm going to tell the story anyway because it's worth the shame! With no space for a waste bin in our compact en suite bathroom, after using dental floss before sleep, I took to dropping it on the floor, to dispose of the day after. (Winnie had never liked me putting it into the toilet either.) The day had finally arrived for my daughters and I to travel to Australia. Pushing against a degree of inertia and apathy, I had eventually acted on Winnie's repeated encouragement during the first medium reading to go there. Although now there was much excitement, my feelings were inevitably mixed, embarking on this adventure without her. Rising from bed to take the few paces to the bathroom, I instantly located the dental floss discarded from the previous night. I had to rub my eyes, and keep steady on my feet. A perfect letter 'W' (Figure 7). Transfixed, staring down in utter amazement, laughing, crying.

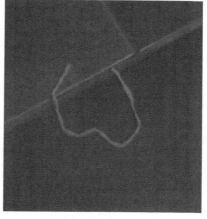

Bittersweet. Regaining some composure, I gently closed the bathroom door with a trembling hand to prevent the chance of one of the cats disturbing this unique gift, to return after breakfast. By then reopening the door, a draught of air passed under it, for a heart shape to be born right before my eyes, like an intimate spectacle performed just for me. *A cherished message from my beloved one, her timing impeccable, as always. What strength it gave me to truly believe she was with us, aware of everything.*

Australia was both spectacular and healing. Being with family and friends in this extraordinary country was just what we needed to regain some faith in the beauty life has to offer, the feeling of peace there almost tangible. Two of my cousins there had experienced much in their lives, both of them wise and spiritually minded, albeit in different ways, and hours of discussion helped me immeasurably. Our friends Richard and Kristy and their children had emigrated to Melbourne a few years earlier, and were devastated by Winnie's passing. I had kept them informed of how we were managing, and of course about all the wonderful signs we'd received. On numerous occasions long before our trip, they voiced their sincere hope for a message of some kind whilst being there together in Australia. Their wish appeared to be fulfilled, to our amused delight. In a pair of Kristy's jeans, a small rip above the knee had gradually enlarged over a few days. While chatting after dinner one evening, with nervous, wide eyes, she now saw how the tear in the fabric had developed into a heart shape.

Winnie had always felt so welcomed and contented at my parents' home, where we visited most weekends with the girls. So it made complete sense that a sign of affection would materialise there, a treasure that was still present eighteen months since it first came into my view. In the living room where all the family usually congregate for gatherings, the heart could be seen in the fireplace, formed by a peeling of the coating on the surrounding bricks. We were unsure for how long it had already been there, which seemed to fit with the approach Winnie had adopted to family life in the latter years – more in the background but always present, caring. *Everywhere we turn, her love remains.*

In October 2014, the wedding of my youngest brother Michael to Roz took place. Their engagement had been announced the year before, and Winnie had been very much looking forward to the occasion and the family celebration. Shortly before in Belgium, Nelly had seen the medium for a second time, and during this reading, having no prior knowledge of the impending event, it was revealed that Winnie would be there with us, joining the family at the ceremony.

On the morning of the marriage, Roz, her mum and brides-maids, including my daughters, were on the verge of excitedly leaving the house for the hairdressers. One in the group then noticed a white feather on the coffee table next to some cups, as if it had been placed there to be noticed. From the various books I'd read, white feathers turning up in unusual places was a sign that many bereaved people had received.

There had been some annoyance for Michael leading up to the big day due to the hired suits having been poorly measured, with no time for changes to be made. It was time for me to check if mine fitted. Unzipping the bag, I laid out the garments on the bed, with Michael standing beside me, still agitated. With a keener eye than usual, he complained, 'Look, and there's a mark on yours!' before I even had the chance to try it on. At first, I thought he was imagining it, but on closer inspection, angling the fabric towards the light from the  window, I too saw the mark. On one of the sleeves, close to the elbow, was the unmistakable shape of a heart (Figure 8). Initial utter disbelief soon turned to an exhilarating, warm feeling that spread through all my family who witnessed it. We all knew what it meant.

We'd hoped for any kind of small message on this unique day when Winnie would be especially missed. But this was beyond my imagination. We hear of many people having lost someone close talk about them 'watching over us from up there', perhaps sadly with only a doubtful flicker of hope that it could be true. We have been lucky enough to have our awareness raised to such an extent, turning a devoted and elemental wish into a dazzling, unwavering belief.

Chapter 5

After: Peace

She loved me. She still loves me. She's still loving me! It's a magical, astounding feeling to realise and comprehend this. And even if I do still live in a different world, one which sometimes feels acutely isolated from the mainstream, what elation to never forget that she, such a beautiful soul, chose me to be her husband to experience whatever may come in this life. I will be forever humbled and honoured to be her special one. It can't be more complete. Every part of my being loves every part of hers.

Everything that had happened since Winnie's passing echoed her character and our harmony. Almost as if it's to be expected that such an in tune relationship should continue to chime audible notes that can somehow traverse the sound barrier.

During another cycling trip close to our home, I halted abruptly to sit at a bench near the edge of a small local lake. Observing the sun emerge from behind the clouds, brilliant beams honed in, as if seeking a direct path to me, reflecting a limitless shoal of stars across the rippling water. I realised that when the shadow passes, and you step into the sunlight, it will always find you, wherever you are.

It's a strange, paradoxical feeling that whilst my heart will be permanently scarred by her loss, at the same time it has never been fuller, revived and protected by love. Damaged and renewed. My approach to life is more serene, balanced and philo-sophical, a wry smile the backdrop to every situation encoun-tered, a resilient acceptance that things will happen outside our control and understanding. Life, it seems to me, as complex as it can appear, boils down to simple things. For every one of us, from whatever background, a voyage of sometimes extreme and opposite experiences; the challenge to learn how to navigate and progress through calm and storm, gaining wisdom and growing from every situation we are confronted with.

I remembered too that as a child I had a number of recurring out of body experiences of some kind, I now believe them to be. They happened whilst being in a relaxed, natural meditative state, feeling 'spaced out' in a way, but definitely not asleep. In my mind's eye, images of the vast expanse of space appeared, populated by millions of stars. At the same time, an unnerving question was posed, 'Who am I?', as if my consciousness, that voice in my head, was detached from my body.

I still don't understand these experiences, and maybe that is the point. Many things that happen in our lives cannot, and probably should not, always be completely explained. But when the time is right, we can contemplate deeper meanings, to maybe catch a glimpse of what is beneath the iceberg's tip?

My clarity of thought has never been sharper. Before, an elusive mist often seemed to obscure the full view of many situations, leading to indecision and doubt. Now, the perspective is so clear, all the essential elements and priorities of my life recognised, with the understanding of how they fit together, and the confidence to take action. The single most important, anchoring yet liberating reason for this is the knowledge that Winnie believes in me.

Her love has given me new found purpose and conviction to make my own way, sweeping away an inherent lack of self-belief. She has saved my life not once, but twice! 'Before and After'... You might think it impossible to advance and feel reinforced when the love has been so immense. But that is precisely why I feel strengthened and sustained by her. Love never ends, never ceases, is never lost. It remains, healing, uplifting, inspiring, nurturing and guiding us. It's still thriving on a different level, forever positive and glowing bright.

Just over a year after the last time, my daughters and I had another reading with the same medium. Able to make contact with Winnie very quickly, she said, 'Jane,' which I confirmed was her middle name, one that I used all the time. I was told that I seemed to be in a better place, my spirituality and sensitivity flowing more constantly than before. The medium said, 'You always thought that she was the stronger one, but she says it's you. She would not have been able to cope so well.' I replied, 'That's because of all the wonderful signs and messages. She inspires me.' 'She says that you're inspiring her too. You have accepted the situation, and are able to celebrate the memories. She knows that you talk to her, and that you send her messages of love all the time.' *I love the thought that she hears me.* 'You've booked a holiday recently, she's saying.' I confirmed this was correct. 'We're going with Winnie's mum, who's coming over here from Belgium, then we're travelling together.' The medium hadn't known that the family was Belgian. 'She's saying something about France, travelling there for hours and hours on the motorway. Belgique.' The medium looked a little puzzled, and asked me what she had just said? She wasn't familiar with the French word for Belgium. 'She's showing me the journey inside the car, a kind of station wagon. Now she saying, "Gite," that you arrived at a place quite far into the South of France, miles away from anywhere in the countryside. English speaking in France, and growing own vegetables.' (For two consecutive years, we stayed in the Cognac area at the 'Gite du Calme', owned by a lovely English family. And in their garden, they did indeed grow lots of herbs and vegetables. On the first occasion, we did drive all the way from home in our large car, which of course took many hours, and met up with her mum and uncle at the cottage.)

I felt it was significant that these delightful memories from the Gite were recalled. A photo of the view from the idyllic property taken by Winnie has hung in our bathroom for a few years (Figure 9). *I observe it daily, not only to reminisce, but also for succour and assurance, because in the trees I see two hearts, seemingly suspended on the same axis, a reminder that we belong together.*

The morning after the reading, I received the gift of yet

another heart sign! After getting up, the first task was to open the dishwasher for clean crockery to use for breakfast. The first item pulled out from the appliance was a plate to which a piece of red pepper skin had stuck, shaped uncannily like a heart.

As was usual, I shared a transcript of the visit with family and friends, one of whom, Darren, chose his words beautifully in making the comment, 'Lovely. It reads like Winnie is just behind a thick pane of smoky glass. It's like she has true form. She still sees and feels. The references are never bland. They all appear to come from one who knows.'

I have learned that a number of largely insignificant past events at the time later assume meaning and make sense of the future, bestowing perspective. The day I discovered Winnie's pocket notebook was pivotal in the quest for tranquillity. She had been reading a book about counting your blessings, listing many of the joys in her life for which she was grateful. There were no new revelations here, since she had always voiced her appreciation, and shown her affection in many ways. But to witness and to touch the imprint of her words, written by her own hand nine months before passing over, to reconnect with her loving thoughts in those moments, was a gift like no other. They serve as a reminder for me to acknowledge and be grateful for the many good things we have in this life. And it was here that I came upon the words that mean so very much to me, 'De verbondenheid, eenheid, liefde' (connection, unity, love).

The find like a milestone reached in my life, the words feel to be a fundamental, elemental part of me, as she will always be. Could she have ever sensed that her truth, committed to that page, would later guide, and be of incredible support and consequence to her husband?

Winnie's dad Pierre often counselled simply that 'time and patience' ('tijd en geduld') were needed in many situations that arose. Now, years later, I conscientiously follow his wise words of advice, accepting that the path ahead often needs time to be enlightened, evoking the feeling that such learnings are elastic in time, their provenance in the past, while also being meant to serve in the present and future.

Whatever happens in my life, however long I live, I am embraced by the serene belief that Winnie Jane is my home, where I belong, and to whom I will return. Time is the only distance between our reunion.

The very last email from Winnie stored on my computer was found to be unique. Sent from work about three weeks before she became ill, it was signed off in a way that wasn't even noticed at the time. Instead of the typical 'see you tonight love,' she closed with, 'Bye my darling,' a simple phrase that, however, implies an air of parting and finality, which on reflection I'm almost certain she had never used in our written messages before.

In one of her numerous boxes of keepsakes, Winnie had kept a long forgotten gift tag from a Christmas present (a solid bracelet embedded with eye shaped detail) I had given to her some years before. I had written a line from a popular song at the time requesting, 'Just keep your eyes on me, never lose sight of me.' *Now in the present, I feel this is exactly what she is doing for me. She always did her best for her loved ones, and I could not ask for more.*

On the day when we experienced our first subtle connection, for some reason I distinctly remember, hours before the encounter, paying unusual attention to the black suede boots she was wearing, noting how small and dainty they looked. Now those same boots are seen every day, stored at eye level in a wardrobe, never to be given away or worn by another, belonging to this apparently random, yet special flashback, as if this is the place where they were always destined to reside.

Could such arbitrary events be markers traced in time, to be recognised as links between past and present, reassuring reminders of paths taken?

Furthermore, in the photo of Winnie taken on that same day (see page 6), she is wearing a black and white (and grey) checked woollen scarf, which she later kept in drawers directly beneath the print of L'Empire des Lumieres in our home.

Back in the present, and just over a year after Winnie's birth chart reading, I met up with Elizabeth again, with whom I had been in touch when she told me she received a message from Winnie wanting me to have my own chart read! Before starting, Elizabeth told me that she had lived a very vivid dream at 4am that morning in which Winnie came to her, saying she had been travelling and learning languages.

While the dream only seemed to last for a few short moments, many things were communicated. Elizabeth had always believed that life on Earth is like being in school to learn lessons, to practice and develop ourselves, the other side being where we study, rest, reflect and plan the next life to further develop the soul. In the dream, Winnie agreed but also added that we are all learning to be teachers too, and it is important to impart the knowledge we learn to help others to grow. Finally, Winnie had a small ball of bright light in her hand, telling Elizabeth, 'This is how I feel about Andrew.' She then threw the ball of light at Elizabeth's chest, who later told me it was the most wonderful sensation she'd ever experienced at that moment in her dream.

Pure love.

Just as it was during the first reading, when something was said that Winnie particularly agreed with, Elizabeth felt tingling goose bumps on her arm. I too had the same sensation on the top of my head, and wondered if it was on purpose as I often recall when she stroked my head with so much affection while she was actually improving in hospital.

My chart is mostly dominated by the moon and fire signs, and indicates astrological polar opposites, being one of the most challenging patterns. The main learning theme is the notion of attaining everything valued in a life, only then to have nothing. *(The light and the dark...)*

Fire represents high impetus and drive (for things that I believe in). The moon is linked to a person's emotional approach to life, sensitivity, intuition and instinct, spirituality, perception and connection, balancing the fire with feeling. The chart shows deep concern for other people and the need to care for them, and a profound, lasting connection to mother and/or partner. There are aspects associated with travelling, living abroad, and marrying a foreign partner, charted in such a position leading Elizabeth to interpret that Winnie is instrumental in my karmic development (basically meaning striving to achieve balance for long past actions). Certain configurations are associated with loss and death, but also of change, new beginnings, soul searching and legacy. In addition, it suggests that my personal growth is linked to the unearthing of matters, bringing them forward to share, and 'the big picture'. An area of good fortune and good karma is linked to children, meaning my girls are seen as a true gift and blessing. *This, I have always known...*

Elizabeth knew about my plans to write a book, having the strong feeling it would be a very constructive undertaking on many levels. While explaining what inspired me to embark on it (that positive changes must start with individuals, and we can all make a difference in some way), she said afterwards that for the first time ever, she experienced an out of body episode for a few seconds!

You can't imagine how much the insights from this reading with Elizabeth have helped me. Everything makes sense on further reflection, connections made, long existing gaps bridged, and intuitions supported, exploring a fuller understanding of myself, and the depth of my relationship with Winnie.

Meanwhile, yet more instances of love, connection and symbolism were unfolding. On a bike ride, my peripheral vision picked up another heart in the form of a leaf, lying on the damp canal path. However, this time, I rode past, and even though I stopped a few seconds later, I didn't go back to take a photo. Surmising that leaves like this were perhaps nothing out of the ordinary, I decided that it could be one consigned to memory. For the next few days, the thought of the leaf, and why I hadn't taken the opportunity to record the image continually vexed me. Unable to shake off this feeling, I rode back one sunny early morning before work to find the leaf waiting patiently in the same place. On the same way back home, feeling content that I had least satisfied my nagging curiosity, I slowed to meet not two but three white swans, resting motionless on the steaming mirror of water. Reflecting on this beautiful vision of serenity, I wondered whether this was the true reason why I was compelled to return to the leaf. *My gut feeling said that she was, in her own graceful way, intimating that: 'It's alright to love someone else, as well as her.'*

A few months later, Gabrielle and I attended an open day at Leeds University, where she was due to begin her studies in September 2015. At a point in the schedule, there was a sample lecture taking place in one of the largest theatres. A group of around two hundred students and parents made their way to this location, trudging up numerous flights of stairs to slowly filter into the hall, banked with wooden benches. After much shifting up to make space for the last attendees to sit down, the talk started. Listening intently for half an hour, I happened to avert my attention to glance down in front of me. Perfectly aligned with the place I had eventually settled were hearts scored into the wood with a pen. At the end of the lecture, excited by the discovery, I scanned the other rows of benches for more graffiti. From what I could see, and also being able to verify more thoroughly some months later participating in a symposium at the same venue, the three hearts were the only examples to be found in the whole theatre.

A random event with a one in two hundred probability? A lovely coincidence? Or was this episode of apparent chance, incidents that we all encounter, something with concealed structure and purpose, a signpost of significance supposed to be reached and reflected upon?

Our closest friends in Belgium, Jackie and Patrick, had often visited us in England, enjoying wonderful times together. And though the shadow of Winnie's palpable absence was inevitably present, we continued to meet up and maintain our friendship. As always, I encouraged Jackie to choose some of Winnie's clothes for herself, and there was soon to be a christening for one of her granddaughters, so it seemed a good time to delve into the 'treasure chest' that was Winnie's wardrobe. It would mean a great deal to have a little part of her present at this happy event. On that day, our good friend Sarah was also with us, and was delighted to be presented with one of her dresses I thought she'd like. It was touching for them to own and wear anything that belonged to their dear friend, especially when they could easily visualise how lovely she had looked in them. Returning then to our bedroom, I happened to spot a summer dress that hadn't been noticed minutes before. 'This one too,' I thought, as I pulled it out of the wardrobe to show them. At that moment, Sarah had been describing this very same dress to Jackie, commenting how stunning Winnie had looked in it. They smiled in surprised wonder at the garment held in my hand, and at the harmonious timing.

During the summer of 2015, more enchanting heart signs were to cross my path. It started by noticing how a paint chip on my car had developed over time into the unmistakable form of a heart. The next trio of events happened while Nelly was with us during a period of three weeks. While Francesca and I were playing tennis in our garden, at one point I fielded the ball that had rolled along the grass. I'm so glad that before I removed it, I caught sight of a tiny and perfect leaf picked up by the ball on its travels (Figure 10).

A week later in Cyprus, my daughters and I were walking along the rocky south-east coast, while Nelly rested on a nearby bench enjoying the sun's heat. An uneven blend of thousands of stones and pebbles mixed with sand and dust made up the pathway, thus sometimes requiring caution to avoid mishap. Looking down to ensure a good footing for the next step, I placed my sandal right beside a stone perhaps like no other on this trail (Figure 11), and which now resides in our kitchen next to a photo of Winnie.

On the sixth day of our week staying in a villa on Cyprus, after waking early to brilliant sunshine, I decided to change the arrangement of the window blind and curtain in my room, attempting to allow better airflow to combat the already rising heat. In doing so, I came upon a small hole in the blind that hadn't been seen until that point. Closer inspection revealed it to be an inverted heart shape. *Whilst I may not always sense it, as if behind a veil, love is always present, waiting to be found. Perhaps another subtle, almost poetic reminder that love is all around us when we are open and aware.*

Every Father's Day, on behalf of her and the girls, Winnie used to write a card with beautiful words of appreciation for my efforts. Thankfully, I had kept all these precious tokens, and on the day of the occasion in 2015 took them out to read during a quiet moment alone in the evening. Suddenly, I noticed that the design of one of the cards was strikingly similar to that of the notebook I was using to capture ideas for this book. At the time, I had been doubting and deliberating whether to even start the project, and her written words of love, support and appreciation mirrored some of the main messages planned for the book, and the reasons for writing it. *A sign of encouragement to continue, to believe it was the right thing to do? That's what I acted upon...*

After starting writing this book, things continued to happen and be perceived. In the living room, I came upon a lovely symmetrical heart shape made from dust and mud that had collected on the floor. A couple of days earlier, one of Winnie's nieces had given birth to her first child, and Nelly was going to see them on the day I found the heart. Another time, watching the film *Lucy* at home with my daughters, one of the male characters asked, 'Where is she?', at which point his phone received a text saying, 'I am everywhere.' A second later, the halogen lamp in the corner of the room flickered once, and all three of us looked at each other knowingly, the same thought coming to mind.

The date of our tenth wedding anniversary approached, and was to be a day of both joy and melancholy *(for better, for worse)*, as counselled by Nelly, reliving that momentous day like looking in a mirror offering no reflection. But it would be sadder still should we not be able to embrace and enjoy the enduring memories of delight. From major events to everyday smiles, every one is a treasure never to fade away.

On the day before the anniversary, the thought came that I should reminisce by looking through Winnie's numerous boxes of belongings. I had the feeling that something precious could be found. After work, I took my time to pull out all manner of books, especially language dictionaries, smiling, seeing them all signed and dated as she always did. A small box contained various items, including mutual letters during the first difficult months after she had moved to England, and a Valentine's Day card with such tender words expressing her feelings for me. And this was where she kept the wedding cards, and to my surprise, since I'd forgotten about it, some ribbon we'd had specially printed to decorate the wedding cars. As was her way, she'd rolled it up very neatly, and out of learned habit, I unravelled it with equal care, excited to look upon our names, to revive the memories. What I saw surpassed the expectation, for on the back of the ribbon there remained a piece of Blu Tack, almost certainly placed there by Winnie, all those years before to fix the fabric strip to the cars (Figure 12).

I stared at the heart shape for an unknown length of time, imagining her pressing the gum to the ribbon, leaving her fingerprints in time, transporting me back to our happiest day. And with that, the revelation that new memories of Winnie are still being created, guided by her hand, more wonders to be cherished.

Seeing how, as before, I almost always acted with a positive demeanour, people would ask how I was able to cope with such heartbreak. I reflected upon it, which in turn has really helped me when occasionally referring back to the reasons. Most importantly, the responsibility and pleasure of bringing up our daughters, helping them to flourish, is a privilege that defines me, and keeps me grounded.

Quite simply, I'm driven to make Winnie proud of us, for who we are, for what we do and how we achieve it, inspired by her example, whilst adapting our own way. I feel strongly that I owe it to her to live this life as well as I can manage, continuing to appreciate the smallest gifts that life offers, counting blessings, and taking nothing for granted.

Between Winnie and I, love, the most dominant and undying of emotions, overcomes **everything**.

I believe there are no limits to its healing, to the heights it can scale, no frontiers it cannot span.

It finds a way, it flows between us, the unbreakable, eternal wonder that connects us, the miracle that happens every day.

And we'll be together again…

Chapter 6

Ahead

Time draws the horizon slowly, inexorably nearer, almost unnoticed, the vast open sea less daunting, less solitary. Comfort from the rhythm and rise of the tide, waves breaking on land, always ebbing, returning on their perpetual cycle.

I heard it said that a life is perhaps not only about enjoyment, contentment, and the fulfilment of our dreams. Almost fifty years have passed to begin to appreciate this, and only since Winnie's passing. And although I'm fit and well, encountering plenty of happy moments every day while enduring far fewer sombre ones, it's hard to know when I will ever be able to simply describe myself as happy again. There are still questions to address – where to go from here? which path to take? – with the new outlook that inevitably develops after such experiences, seeing the world through different eyes. And what further lessons can be learned?

My priority is to be the best dad, son, son-in-law, brother, godfather and friend, in particular to further understand and develop my role as a father in my daughters' lives. Sharing what's most important in my life – love, compassion, gratitude. Experiencing, learning, and teaching. *Winnie would want this...*

I'm not waiting for, nor rushing to search for anything. Time and patience need to run their courses. I'll continue to rely on instinct and intuition to guide the way, possibly crossing paths with people sharing their own stories, with whom I can learn and grow together. To illustrate, the first months after Winnie's passing were a period of frequent insecurity, my fertile mind at times unable to restrain premature thoughts of the intimidating future. I had been repeatedly troubled by the impossible prospect of happiness without Winnie, of being able to share life with another. At the same time, the random idea arrived that I wanted to know the number of the day in the year she died. Day 259, the 16th September 2013. It then just seemed a natural next step to make the link with the book I was reading at the time, *The Celestine Prophecy* (Reference 1). What I read on page 259 resonated with me perfectly, arriving at the time when really needed. It revealed that the most rewarding relationships are founded first on friendship rather than physical attraction. Friends, I could deal with, not replacements.

I'll continue to be guided by heart rather than head, good intentions and reverence the only road to peace for me. In all important situations, my heart always has the casting vote, feeling always outweighs thinking. I'll be mindful to live in the present, paying heightened attention when feeling moments of love, savouring and reflecting on them, aware to avoid the looming trap of sleepwalking through this often hectic life. Reliving the sheer pleasure of wonderful memories will be a vital stream in my life ahead, connecting with senses and feelings from the past to be back in the moment, a mental safety net to prevent falling too low. I see them as conduits of positive energy, coursing through consciousness, readily available whenever needed to uplift. I'll strive to find the right balance of remembering and learning from the past, while looking to the future without neglecting the here and now.

On the day that would have been Winnie's fiftieth birthday, I walked into the bathroom to find to my surprise, given it was the end of December, a ladybird alive on the wall. The significance only became clear the day after when I decided to tidy the little office, the state of which had always irritated her in the past. Among the items to clear from the floor, under some documents there was a box of Winnie's belongings that I'd placed there and forgotten a couple of months before, intending to take a look. The design of the box was covered with large printed ladybirds! Instantly recognising this as a lovely reminder to discover what gifts it may reveal, I sat down to find out. The treasure trail led to one of her most personal journals, describing her deepest thoughts during her late teenage years. Then it jumped right to the end of August 2001, about ten weeks after she had arrived in England to be with me. Those times had been especially hard, adapting to her new life, and her words (see below), written beguilingly in English rather than her mother tongue, shook my emotions, having not understood the full extent of her pain, now echoing prophetically back to me:

I felt alone and lonely. It took me quite some time to realise that distance doesn't change love or friendship. I had to be ready to let go before being able to love them even more – from within me. All those whom I love are in my heart night and day, and they should be able to feel it. I will be OK from now on.

Led to Winnie's own sound advice from another time, characteristically wise and pragmatic, it will guide me onward, her voice never far away.

I still come upon signs and messages of love from time to time, like the heart shape made from loose threads found on the stairs. It was Valentine's Day, 2016. I don't ever remember explicitly asking for any of them. They are just there, never expected nor taken for granted, and always bringing joy.

Whilst this book tells a very personal story, I feel strongly compelled to share it with others in need. Not everyone will experience what I have in receiving and perceiving signs when a loved one has departed. Writing it has felt so natural, and has flowed effortlessly, as if I have been long prepared for it. Even if you never knew Winnie nor me, I hope it will stir emotions, open eyes to new insights, in some small way encourage further reflection and understanding of our purposes. I believe the writing of Winnie's book to be a principal one of mine. And I hope it serves to delve deeper to discover and listen to your intuition, learning to trust your inner source of untapped wisdom, so easily drowned out by the noise of modern life. My wish is that some of the stories and reflections may engender a resonant, familiar echo in your own life. Maybe it can help to recognise and accept the ever-present duality in our lives, the sunshine and shadow, bitter and sweet. And perhaps not to be afraid of death. Every day, we hear about taking care of our physical and mental health. Winnie's book is about elevating spiritual health.

It may sound strange, but since Winnie passed on, and after all that has happened, I don't feel lonely in the normal sense of the word. One of my friends, Hilde, who has been helping me with this book, commented, 'You walk around like someone who knows they're never alone.' That's true. I don't know what I'd do without her...

The End. *The End? I don't think so...*

De verbondenheid, eenheid, liefde (Figure 13).

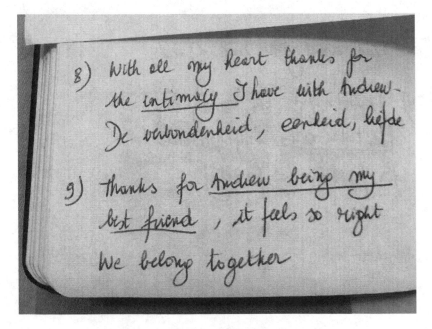

References

1. Redfield, J., 1994, *The Celestine Prophecy*. Imprint 2009. London: Transworld Publishers.

BOOKS

6th Books
ALL THINGS PARANORMAL

Investigations, explanations and deliberations on the paranormal, supernatural, explainable or unexplainable. 6th Books seeks to give answers while nourishing the soul: whether making use of the scientific model or anecdotal and fun, but always beautifully written.
Titles cover everything within parapsychology: how to, lifestyles, alternative medicine, beliefs, myths and theories.
If you have enjoyed this book, why not tell other readers by posting a review on your preferred book site? Recent bestsellers from 6th Books are:

The Afterlife Unveiled
What the Dead Are Telling us About Their World!
Stafford Betty
What happens after we die? Spirits speaking through mediums know, and they want us to know. This book unveils their world...
Paperback: 978-1-84694-496-3 ebook: 978-1-84694-926-5

Spirit Release
Sue Allen
A guide to psychic attack, curses, witchcraft, spirit attachment, possession, soul retrieval, haunting, deliverance, exorcism and more, as taught at the College of Psychic Studies.
Paperback: 978-1-84694-033-0 ebook: 978-1-84694-651-6

The Miracle Workers Handbook
Seven Levels of Power and Manifestation of the Virgin Mary
Sherrie Dillard
Learn how to invoke the Virgin Mary's presence, communicate
with her, receive her grace and miracles and become a miracle
worker.
Paperback: 978-1-84694-920-3 ebook: 978-1-84694-921-0

Divine Guidance
The Answers You Need to Make Miracles
Stephanie J. King
Ask any question and the answer will be presented, like a direct
line to higher realms... *Divine Guidance* helps you to regain
control over your own journey through life.
Paperback: 978-1-78099-794-0 ebook: 978-1-78099-793-3

The End of Death
How Near-Death Experiences Prove the Afterlife
Admir Serrano
A compelling examination of the phenomena of Near-Death
Experiences.
Paperback: 978-1-78279-233-8 ebook: 978-1-78279-232-1

The Psychic & Spiritual Awareness Manual
A Guide to DIY Enlightenment
Kevin West
Discover practical ways of empowering yourself by unlocking
your psychic awareness, through the Spiritualist and New Age
approach.
Paperback: 978-1-78279-397-7 ebook: 978-1-78279-396-0

An Angels' Guide to Working with the Power of Light
Laura Newbury
Discovering her ability to communicate with angels, Laura
Newbury records her inspirational messages of guidance and
answers to universal questions.
Paperback: 978-1-84694-908-1 ebook: 978-1-84694-909-8

The Audible Life Stream
Ancient Secret of Dying While Living
Alistair Conwell
The secret to unlocking your purpose in life is to solve the
mystery of death, while still living.
Paperback: 978-1-84694-329-4 ebook: 978-1-78535-297-3

Beyond Photography
Encounters with Orbs, Angels and Mysterious Light Forms!
John Pickering, Katie Hall
Orbs have been appearing all over the world in recent years.
This is the personal account of one couple's experience of this
new phenomenon.
Paperback: 978-1-90504-790-1

Blissfully Dead
Life Lessons from the Other Side
Melita Harvey
The spirit of Janelle, a former actress, takes the reader on a
fascinating and insightful journey from the mind to the heart.
Paperback: 978-1-78535-078-8 ebook: 978-1-78535-079-5

Does It Rain in Other Dimensions?
A True Story of Alien Encounters
Mike Oram
We have neighbors in the universe. This book describes one
man's experience of communicating with other-dimensional

and extra-terrestrial beings over a 50-year period.
Paperback: 978-1-84694-054-5

Dreamer
20 Years of Psychic Dreams and How They Changed My Life
Andrew Paquette
A ground-breaking, expectation-shattering psychic dream book
unlike any other.
Paperback: 978-1-84694-502-1 ebook: 978-1-84694-728-5

Electronic Voices: Contact with Another Dimension?
Anabela Mourato Cardoso
Career diplomat and experimenter Dr Anabela Cardoso covers
the latest research into Instrumental Transcommunication and
Electronic Voice Phenomena.
Paperback: 978-1-84694-363-8

The Hidden Secrets of a Modern Seer
Cher Chevalier
An account of near death experiences, psychic battles between
good and evil, multidimensional experiences and Demons and
Angelic Helpers.
Paperback: 978-1-84694-307-2 ebook: 978-1-78099-058-3

Spiritwalking
The Definitive Guide to Living and Working with the Unseen
Poppy Palin
Drawing together the wild craft of the shamanic practitioner
and the wise counsel of the medium or psychic, *Spiritwalking*
takes the reader through a practical course in becoming an
effective, empathic spiritwalker.
Paperback: 978-1-84694-031-6

What Dwells Within: A Study of Spirit Attachment
Jayne Harris, Dan Weatherer
A book discussing the work of leading paranormal investigator
Jayne Harris and her studies into haunted objects.
Paperback: 978-1-78535-032-0 ebook: 978-1-78535-033-7